Famous in Their Twenties

Famous in Their Twenties

by

CHARLOTTE HIMBER

CT
220
H5
1970

Essay Index Reprint Series

 BOOKS FOR LIBRARIES PRESS
FREEPORT, NEW YORK

STANDARD BOOK NUMBER:
8369-1659-X

LIBRARY OF CONGRESS CATALOG CARD NUMBER:
79-111837

PRINTED IN THE UNITED STATES OF AMERICA

Contents

Foreword—1970

TWENTY FIVE YEARS AGO I talked with the famous people you'll read about in this book. The teenagers of that day knew them well, but to you they are probably strangers.

Why, then, do I think you will want to read about them? My answer is that as each of these individuals talks of himself you will recognize a personality that is representative. You'll recognize, in the famous runner Leslie McMitchell, the kind of person whose goal is to cover distance on foot faster than anyone in the whole country had yet done.

What sort of person is this? What motivates him? This is as revealing about today's famous runners, James Ryan, or Poncho Gonzales, whom you probably know.

Alec Templeton tells in this book how it is to live almost entirely through musical experiences. Today's youth, listening with excitement to Paul McCartney, Joan Baez, Bob Dylan, Van Cliburn — or to the singers of bubble-gum music — will, if anything, understand even better than the youth of Templeton's day, the powerful message these famous people can deliver through music. Templeton was, in fact, ahead of his time. The young people today are more attuned to him, in understanding that music like Bach and Bop are one and the same. Such music is an expression of the soul of man releasing feelings that mount and swell in the complications of his daily living.

The tennis champion described in this book, Alice Marble, is probably not known to you, but tennis is now having a big comeback. Arthur Ashe, Jr. and Nancy Richey are famous personalities of our day who are facing the same challenges that Alice Marble faced.

And so it goes. Each youth carries within him the seeds of a tremendous potential — the same seeds that sprout to fame in one or another marked personality by some mystic combination of genes and chance. Read about these famous people as though you know them as your contemporaries, or as elements of yourself — for they are, indeed, Everyman, and they and you share feelings, fantasies and fulfillment, no matter how you use your time in each day's activities.

Charlotte Himber
10/69

Associate Director
Community Affairs Department
National Council of YMCAs

Foreword

PEOPLE WHO HEARD ABOUT THIS BOOK in preparation kept asking me: "What gave you the idea of writing stories of boys and girls who became headliners while they were still in their twenties?"

This is how it happened: I attended a national conference of young boys—the National Hi-Y organization of the Young Men's Christian Association. A thousand boys listened to platform speakers during the five-day session. The speaker who drew the greatest round of applause was the thirty-two-year-old Mayor of Milwaukee, who spoke of the famous young men who created American history. He said:

"To impress you with the ability of young men like yourselves, let us look back at some of the men who led the country in 1776: Alexander Hamilton was eighteen when he first became active in leadership of the colonies; James Madison was twenty-four; James Monroe was seventeen; John Marshall was twenty; Patrick Henry and John Hancock were each twenty-nine when they signed the Declaration; George Washington was twenty-one when he completed his mission to the French. . . ."

The boys listened to this testament of youth with great satisfaction. Their loud applause was a stirring demonstration of youth's wish to be taken into account. That was the sort of thing they were interested in. They listened and understood, and were inspired.

This speaker had cited examples of men who did their work centuries ago. Why not, I thought, do homage to the men and women of our own times who are giving their talents to improve the lot of their fellow man even in the current crisis, and who are blazing trails for a better civilization to come? To get the characters for inclusion in such a book, many boys and girls were cashayed into consultation, and lists were formulated. Some adults were allowed a peek at the lists, but their suggestions were not honored unless they were endorsed by the majority of adolescents who were my consultants.

Some of the characters portrayed here have now grown out of their twenties, and one has recently died. Many of them, however, are still in their twenties. All of them were chosen because my "editorial board" of young people wanted them.

Getting to see the subjects selected was not difficult, for I found them all eager to co-operate on a project that was conceived for youth. They, too, entered into the spirit of the plan to let youth talk to youth. The outcome of these ten interviews is this book, which contains ten stories about people who were successful in spite of their genius.

Many boys and girls are shot straight to the pinnacle of fame in their early twenties, and that is their tragedy, for they are not able to sustain themselves at that dizzy height for long. The qualities of genius that develop into prolonged ability and service to mankind are qualities inherent in every one of us. Even without special talents, many average men have done remarkably well with common traits and uncommon zeal. In my interviews with these exceptional men and women, and in my scrutiny of the step-by-step development of their careers in the various fields of art, science, and industry, I found certain characteristics repeatedly present that seemed to have more to do with their achievements than with their talents.

All the people interviewed love to work. In each case, the goal has not been to be famous, but merely to be allowed to work in a chosen field. They work many more hours than the average man, and regardless of whether their work will net them any kind of remuneration.

They are persistent. They expect to stick to a job at any cost, and they subject themselves to great hardships in order to continue on the task set for themselves, never counting the cost.

They are self-confident. Nobody seems able to discourage them in their self-appointed tasks. They are perfectly certain that their vision is true and that their aim will be achieved in the face of handicap, disapproval, or even ridicule.

They are happy. Neither money nor any material possessions have anything to do with their happiness. Margaret Bourke-White is supremely happy in a below-zero temperature, taking a picture standing on a steeple a thousand feet above ground, while three men help her hold her camera against the wind. The Bukers are happy dodging mosquitos in the steaming jungle country below the Burma, tending horribly deformed lepers. Daniel Poling is happy doubled over in old mines, mingling with the weary miners in an atmosphere of sweat and toil, getting the material for his exposé of the steel industry. And so it goes.

The careers of these men and women are not held up as models. They have made mistakes and expect to make more. I have tried to picture them truthfully, so that you can read about their shortcomings as well as their triumphs. There is no caution against their mistakes, for I have no fear that you will seize upon those for emulation.

Most of them succeeded in an era of depression. They ignored the depression and went to work. The way they went to work suggests how today's young people can find their work in the equally difficult times they now face and will face tomorrow. They were people who might have started out in an entirely different field and still have succeeded. Not luck, influence, or talent would have availed them one whit if they had not employed self-discipline and developed to fullest capacity those common characteristics with which we are all endowed.

It has been fun to talk with these kindly, delightful, and exuberant people. I hope you get as much fun reading about them.

New York
May, 1942

CHARLOTTE HIMBER

He Sees by Music

ALEC TEMPLETON

A<small>S</small> I <small>STEPPED OVER THE THRESHOLD</small> into the hotel suite where Alec Templeton rose to greet me and shake my hand, I stepped right out of my own narrow orbit into an unfamiliar world. Templeton was gay in a heady environment where music is almost the perpetual subject of conversation. The radio was playing softly. He could listen and get every note while carrying on a vigorous and lively conversation with me and checking attentively his wife's telephoning. These activities were so harmonized in his own symphonic style of living that there was no sense of confusion. As we talked, I caught and thrilled to the sheer melody of his genius, while the other sounds in the room furnished an accompaniment like cellos and bass violas in an orchestra.

English-born, Templeton rhapsodizes constantly over modern American composers.

"*Porgy and Bess* is what I look upon as a strictly musical opera—perhaps the greatest American opera. It is not just a light operetta at all," he said. "History was made when the Philharmonic Society of New York permitted Jerome Kern to appear with them in Carnegie Hall. He and Cole Porter are two of the most marvelous composers in the world, not only because they write hits that everybody enjoys—like the five-and-ten-cent-store composers—but because their music, to the ears of true musicians, is full of the most glorious melody. Pieces like *The Way You Look Tonight, Begin the Beguine, I've Got You under My Skin*, those are things that could have been written by Rachmaninoff. Gershwin was even going further. Goodness knows what he would have written if he were alive today. He was the most experimental of any of the modern composers."

"I will never forget the first time I heard Gershwin's *Rhapsody in Blue*. It was about 1924. I was sitting in the dormitory in school, in Worcestershire, England. I was all alone up there, with a pair of headphones on my ears. There was a man downstairs who had a radio, and I could listen through my headphones. The broadcasting was from the Savoy Hotel in London, with the Orpheum band playing—that was the Whiteman band of England. This represented a very unusual kind of broadcast, for their feature was the new Gershwin number from America. It was a wonderful experience. It was the first time I heard a work that at last had combined the classical and jazz, and I could hear how the audience at the Savoy took a terrific liking to it. But I knew that no one in my circle would know it, and I never spoke of it to anyone. I just hoped that maybe some day someone would mention it to me.

"I was studying classical music at the time, but I was absorbing popular music from the early days of ragtime, drinking it all in on the quiet. I had Whiteman's early records. It was not until two years after I first heard the broadcast that someone asked me whether I had ever heard that experimental composition by Gershwin. We were at a friend's house, and this person told me there was a record of it. I bought it at once, and I played it and played it when nobody was around, until I knew it backward. Then

I ventured to play it to people, and at first they were afraid to accept it. It was so modern and so peculiar, and when I'd inflict the record on them, and they heard that opening clarinet, they would ask in amazement: 'What is that?' It is only within the last four years that people are beginning to recognize it as a truly great work."

Alec Templeton talks in a lilting, rhythmic pattern. He repeats phrases in a resonant, throaty voice, first soft and then loud—like a Bach fugue—and comes to a sudden stop. In the quiet of one of his stops, I had a queer feeling. It came over me with a poignant sense of my own affliction that it was I who was blind, not this musician. He dwells in the pure, clear atmosphere of sound. My own field of sensation is muddied by interfering and discordant pictures. For the rest of the interview, I groped for light while he basked in the bright glory of his music.

It is said of Mozart that he composed music when he was so young that, in order to play the several notes to form a chord, he tried to use the tip of his nose. Alec, at four, tried to do the same thing with the aid of his elbows. His musical career was then already two years old. At two, he listened to the sound of the church bells outside his door, and climbing up on the piano seat, he picked over the notes until he could duplicate this sound. Before he was five, he could correct his older sister's playing. Shortly thereafter, still unaware that there was such a thing as the sense of sight (for his family had carefully prevented this knowledge from getting to him), he directed a choir of his playmates. He would compose music for some special occasion, and teach it to them part by part. It was not until he was eight years old that someone outside his own home used the word "blind" to him, and he came to realize that he was different. By this time, his personality was set. He was an active, vital, interested, and happy child. He dwelt in a musical world of his own making, although his early compositions were not recorded. He studied the piano, and in a very short time it was obvious that the boy had uncommon ability.

The Templetons farmed land owned by Lord and Lady Plymouth, in Cardiff, Wales. At twelve, when Alec won a contest for one of his compositions, there was much publicity by the British Broadcasting Company. Only a short time after that, he won against twenty thousand participants in a piano contest sponsored by the London *Daily Express*. Leading musicians predicted a brilliant future, and he was sought by concert managers, music clubs, and orchestras. The family left the farm and went to London to live, where Alec was enabled to get instruction by means of scholarships at the Royal Academy.

The boy learned to play by listening to music, often to phonograph records. That was how he had learned his contest piece. There are Braille texts of music, but Templeton scorns them. "They're so slow," he explained impatiently. "It took me weeks to learn a piece by Braille that I could have learned in an afternoon by listening to it." He is abnormally quick, and the Braille system was not meant for such as he.

It is easy to guess, as one listens to him talk, how swift and sure is his thinking. One wonders whether his musical development might not have been impeded by the confusion of sight. His hearing memory is magnificent. A story often told about him concerns an occasion when the violinist, Nathan Milstein, was giving a concert in Chicago. The story has been told in several different versions, but I got the facts from his manager, Stanley North.

Alec was unhappy at having to miss the concert because of a rehearsal for his own broadcast. But that evening he was invited to a small party with Milstein and other musicians. As usually happens, they "relaxed" by making music for themselves. Finally, Milstein turned to Templeton and said: "Why don't *you* give us something now?" One of the guests suggested that he accompany Milstein with Lalo's *Symphonie Espagnole*, which the violinist had performed only that very afternoon at the concert. "I heard that piece once or twice, but it was several years ago," Alec replied. "I don't know whether I remember it, but I'll try." Mischa Mischakoff followed the score while the two men played. When the performance was over, he announced to the room, with tears of admiration in his eyes: "Alec played it perfectly, with just one mistake. But I really think that mistake was an improvement on the original."

Just before he left for London, Alec was studying piano with Margaret Humphrey, in Cardiff. He remembers that one of the biggest thrills of his youth was the time Sir Thomas Beecham gave a concert at Cardiff with the London Symphony Orchestra. He went with his teacher. "The program would be considered quite popular now, but for me it was a momentous occasion, for I had never heard a real symphonic number before. It was Beethoven's *Fifth Symphony*—I was thrilled, for I had only known light orchestral pieces and the music of outdoor band concerts."

When he went to London, Templeton had the opportunity of hearing more of these classical, symphonic numbers. From the age of sixteen to twenty-five, he toured England, giving classical concerts, but his career as a concert player of serious music was interrupted by his own special art form, known as "musical portraiture" and improvisation. Its first impetus came when he gave a performance attended by the American jazz-band leader, Jack Hylton, whose new American music had taken Paris by storm and invaded the entire Continent. He gave Templeton a contract and brought him to the United States, and before long the Englishman's popularity as a proponent of the American musical art form enabled him to make great headway as a soloist.

Now, we Americans are an odd mixture of bombast and modesty. We produce music that roars and barks and bursts into excited wails. But we continue to be timid and apologetic about "the jazz idiom." We like our music, but we don't think it is terribly important. Then along comes an Englishman who has won our respect for his presentation of the "safe" old classics, and when *he* tells us we are producing art, we raise our heads a bit less fearfully. The American audiences were enthusiastic and grateful to Templeton for his understanding rendition of Gershwin, Jerome Kern, Ferde Grofe, and Cole Porter, as well as for his playing of Debussy, whose music he adores.

It took courage on his part to pioneer with these concerts, but by this time Templeton was confident of his own musical taste and had the insight to credit American audiences with the alertness and ability to understand new musical forms. He made his own vital contribution to the jazz idiom by a great variety of humorous records. Very few people are successfully funny in music, so that Templeton's gayety stands as a unique contribution. Among these records are such satires as *Impressions of Old-fashioned Italian Opera,* in which he mocks the traditional prima donna and the leading tenor; *Shortest Wagnerian Opera,* or *Through the Ring, Tristan, and Tannhäuser in Three Minutes,* which is balm to the ears of the anti-

Wagnerians and yet delights the large circle of Wagner enthusiasts. He took the catchy tune of *The Music Goes 'Round and 'Round* and treated it in a single record as a subject for a Mozart piano sonata, as Johann Strauss would have played it in a Viennese waltz and as Handel would have written it into a grand oratorio. But he ridicules without rancor, for the music is always too delicious and satisfying to cause hard feelings. His melodious ironies, as well as all his playing, appeal to musicians and plain folk alike. *Time* says of him that he not only can swing Bach, but can make Bach swing.

When Templeton went on the radio in 1939, he won six million listeners in two months. I have met people several days after one of these broadcasts, and they were still telling one another how much fun they had listening to Alec Templeton. As one friend put it: "You know I never laugh out loud at performances of any kind—movies or theater or opera—but when I heard that fellow play the piano, I just let out a big loud, belly laugh. He sure did get me!"

Because of his handicap, Templeton has been denied the satisfaction of gratifying any of his longings directly. Always he had to rely on someone's good will and understanding. But having to curb his impatience through the years of his childhood has not made him bitter. To the public, he appears amiable and unworried. Actually, he has had to exercise unusual discipline to maintain this outward calm, since his personal problems, in the management of an active public career, have been far more difficult than for the average man. He has seen to it that no hint of these disturbances has ever affected the people who attend his concerts for peace of mind and amusement.

Templeton is an interesting man to watch. He has so

much energy that he does not remain seated for very long. As he talks, he employs his whole body expressively. When I asked him about his hobbies, he gave a comical demonstration of himself on a horse last year for the first time in his life, using the upholstered chair as a bucking bronco. In exuberant spirits, he jumps out of his chair, stands up and turns around in the middle of the room as he talks.

He appears hearty and healthy, although he says he doesn't exercise much. He probably does not need to, judging from the way he moves about in daily conversation. He likes swimming. But his real hobby is collecting music boxes, or anything else that chimes and plays. Friends send him these from all over the world.

Alec Templeton enjoys fame and success because of his rare ability, but his gift makes its demands. He speaks regretfully of the fact that rarely, because of his career as a musician, does he possess a home of his own—an address that is not a hotel address. He loves New York, particularly because he has so many friends there; but no place has endeared itself to him like California, because there he once had a place he thought of as home, where he knew his way around in familiar surroundings.

He found a kinship with Americans that induced him to apply for American citizenship almost as soon as he arrived in this country. He will go back to England to visit, he thinks, and to try to "sell American music." He has already helped to do that for us all over the world by his rare recordings, but he still thinks that this wonderful American idiom is "forbidden music" in many snobbish European circles, and it is his ambition to take it out of that realm. He thinks the war may do a great deal in this respect, for the allied armies and navies will be lifted in spirit by our melodies, and even the civilian populations will have their morale bolstered by the buoyant grace of jazz. Because morale is one of the most important weapons of war, he believes that anything that will build it up will become of increasing value.

"I have heard that you do musical portraits of people, according to your impressions of them. Can you describe that process?" I asked.

"Certainly. You see, everybody is in a certain key—either flat, sharp, or natural. After I decide on the key for a person, I play him according to whether he is gay, quiet, solemn, and so forth."

In attesting to the uncanny accuracy of these musical portrayals, his wife says that frequently Templeton detects and "plays" characteristics in a person whom he knows but casually that are revealed to friends of long standing only over a considerable time.

Templeton married Juliett Vaiani, a singer, in 1940. "Julie" was with us most of the time during the interview. She shook my hand in a warm, positive greeting, and then became as unobtrusive as possible. Occasionally, by a gesture or a word with Alec, she revealed the sincerity and solicitude that have brought him so much new joy.

Templeton is kind and gentle, and provokes those same qualities in those about him by his own affability. Never does one get the impression that his disposition has been warped because of his lack of sight. "What I can't have, I don't think about" is his philosophy. Yet there is one thing he wants desperately and that he does permit himself to think about often, for he will probably get it: He wants a chance to play his own newly composed symphony,

Rhapsody Harmonique, with the New York Philharmonic Orchestra. "That and Gershwin's *Rhapsody in Blue,*" he adds. He thinks the Philharmonic is the greatest symphony orchestra and Toscanini the greatest conductor. Having once heard Toscanini conduct the Philharmonic in Beethoven's *Eroica,* he maintains that Toscanini spoiled him for anybody else.

I rose to go. The radio announced a number by Sibelius. This reminded Templeton that it was hearing Sibelius that had somehow inspired him to write his own first symphony. "Sibelius somehow makes me want to compose." He is full of touching, unusual reactions like that, and genuinely unrestrained in telling about them. It was hard to leave that room where I felt so thoroughly at home in the atmosphere created by the musician. In little over an hour I had learned to "see" into his dazzling realm of melody, and I disliked getting back to my own dim orbit.

From Elocution to Exploration

LOWELL THOMAS

To MANY PEOPLE, Lowell Thomas is a voice—a voice that swiftly chronicles adventure the world over, tense but orderly, as impersonal as a meteor. You ought to see him. He isn't one bit like that. Of medium height, slender, he speaks very softly, looking around the room as he thinks of what he is going to say. Then, with a friendly, innocent expression, he suddenly directs his gaze on the person whom he is addressing, curious and eager, like a child.

For ten years Lowell Thomas has begun his fifteen-minute news broadcast on the radio with a genteel, "Good evening, everybody," and then launched into a whirlwind of comment on the day's events. Many of you have heard him in the movies, too, recounting the week's high lights of world news. His regular appearances throughout the years on the same radio station, at the same hour, are a great change from the life he once lived—a life of throbbing adventure and travel. Have you ever wondered how he manages to pronounce the strange foreign names and places on the radio so glibly? It is because he has probably lived in the distant land he is describing, heard the native tongue spoken, and hobnobbed with native rulers in their royal regalia. His speech does indeed carry this conviction. He can pronounce "Amanullah," "Waziristan," "Addis Ababa," or "Tobruk" as familiarly as we say "New York" or "Chicago."

11

Lowell Thomas has been around. He was a newsboy at ten, a gold miner at eleven, a reporter in his early teens. All through his childhood, he rubbed shoulders with romance and adventure in the fantastic environment of the Cripple Creek mines. He spent a boyhood that any lad would give his eye teeth to emulate. He attributes his success as an explorer, author, and news commentator to a remarkable combination of lucky circumstances. But you will see how he has shown a rare talent for making the most out of those "breaks," as he calls them.

To begin with, Lowell was really lucky in his parents. His father was a physician trained as a mining surgeon. By profession, the elder Thomas fitted into the Cripple Creek mining town, but he was not otherwise representative of it. Cripple Creek, Colorado, has an altitude of ten thousand feet. In its rare atmosphere, blown by a dry, cool wind, the rocks lie bare and gaunt, silent sentries of the veins of gold that elude the heady adventurer. The men that climbed to Cripple Creek and dwelt there in temporary shacks were hard men, of rough courage, uncultured but for the rich color of experiences gathered in their travels across the country in search of gold. With no other interest or ambition, they lived a crude life, full of daring and adventure.

Lowell was eight years old when his parents came to this town from Woodington, Ohio, in 1900. They had both been country schoolteachers, but his father changed to surgery. He settled in Cripple Creek, where frequent mining accidents placed him and his family in close contact with the residents of the community. In their home the Thomases maintained an atmosphere of culture and refinement, having brought with them a library of three thousand books. Lowell's earliest recollections of family life dwell upon his father's tireless efforts to teach him perfect diction and voice projection. But, as he stepped out through the door of this well-regulated home, the son sought to become part of the anomalous life of a mining town. Wandering about with a stack of newspapers to sell gave the ten-year-old admittance to gambling halls and saloons, and led him to drift between the shacks and old shafts, where he would stop to listen to miners recounting their adventures.

"How would you describe the type of man who is a miner, Mr. Thomas?" I asked.

"You mean a gold miner, don't you?" he corrected. "Not just any miner. A gold miner is of a race apart. He is first of all an adventurer. He is not trying to get rich. He follows the yellow metal in search of something as intangible as the horizon. He braves dangers and squanders fortunes wherever there is hope of its discovery. Nothing else is important to him. He may have started out in life as an engineer, an agriculturist, a student—any number of things—but he has abandoned every other aspiration in the hope of finding gold. In his singleness of purpose and the lack of acquisitiveness attached to it, he differs in kind from all men, even from all other types of miners."

These were the men who fired the boy's imagination. He sought their company everywhere, and fed on their tales. On days when there was no school he took a book of adventure stories under his arm and went off to a mountain tunnel that he called his pirate cave. There he burned fires of pine cones and read till the flames died down, dreaming of the day when his time would come.

"Did you realize that your family differed sharply from the others?"

"Oh, of course."

"Did your father object to your mingling with the miners?"

"Not a bit. He knew I loved to be with them, and didn't worry about the environment. As a matter of fact, as soon as I was old enough to be allowed around the mines at all, I worked with the men."

"From what you have told me, I gather that your family was not pressed for money. How is it that you worked even before your teens?"

"Everybody worked," Thomas said casually. "I did what all the fellows did in Cripple Creek."

The refining influence of a cultured home environment could not be dispelled by these worldly contacts. When Thomas' father made a family hobby of good speech and delivery he may have been relying upon these outward manifestations of a neat and orderly character to serve as a bulwark against rougher influences. A student of religion and philosophy, he also taught his son to understand that goodness can be expressed in a mine tunnel as well as in the words of a minister preaching a Sunday sermon. He believed that religion could be expressed through any aspect of daily life, and that no truly religious person picks his way among men according to their particular denomination.

To this day, Lowell Thomas and his family attend a non-denominational church in their community, which he describes as "the most unique church of its kind in existence." He is so enthusiastic about the subject that he interrupted our interview to expound the virtues of his church. It is situated in a small village in the State of New York. "Everybody goes!" he said "A wealthy man left money for a church to be built on Quaker Hill, with the proviso that it was to be non-denominational. Then an odd thing happened. Because it bears no denominational label, that church has so endeared itself in the community that people of every faith, as well as people of no professed faith at all, attend regularly." That is the kind of church Lowell Thomas likes. His son, a typically modern adolescent, attends with him.

Who's Who records with stark brevity that Lowell Thomas went to four universities within four years, collecting a degree from each. I was curious to know how he had hurdled over college campuses, from Indiana, across the country as far east as Princeton, gathering degrees as he went. His description of these crowded, restless years, throughout his late adolescence and into his early twenties, so characteristically portray the man that his story is worth quoting almost as fully as he gave it to me:

"I went to Valparaiso University in northern Indiana ('the poor man's Harvard') because I could work my way. When I arrived, without saying anything to anybody, I enrolled in both Freshman and Sophomore classes. After a month or so, they called me on the carpet and told me that was against the rules. However, I pleaded with them to let me continue until such time as I failed to make good in my work. The result was that I finished the regular four-year course in two years, and got both my Bachelor's and Master's degrees. At the same time, I paid my own way, working as a waiter, cook, and real-estate salesman.

"Upon returning to the mining camp in Colorado, I found that my college training had equipped me to go to work in the mines, on the business end of a pick and shovel, and that was about all.

"However, a month or so later, the editor of a local daily paper offered me a job as a reporter. In a short time, they made me City Editor, and shortly after that put me in charge of the paper. Then some financiers from Denver came up and launched a rival daily, and offered me more money to run that. When I decided to accept the offer, the first paper hired an exceedingly energetic young lawyer and former reporter to take my place. For the rest of that year, we were rival editors in hot competition. His name was Ralph Carr, and he is the present Governor of Colorado.

"At the end of a year, I decided I couldn't get much further in newspaper work in that mining camp, and so I took a year's post-graduate work at the University of Denver. They were reluctant to accept my credits from Valparaiso because I had pushed through the former in two years. I stayed at Denver University a year, working my way by means of a full-time job on a Denver paper, and the following spring received two more degrees, again a Bachelor's and a Master's degree.

"After a summer of ranching in the Southwest, I made up my mind to return East and study law. I had always intended to enter the legal profession. Again wanting to work my way, I got a job on an evening newspaper and enrolled at Chicago Kent College of Law, where I studied law at night. A week or two after entering, they put me on the faculty, in temporary charge of the Department of Forensic Oratory, pinch-hitting for someone else. The result was that I held down the job for two years. At the end of that time, I was offered a position in the largest law firm in America. But by then I was becoming puzzled about the future. Without being fully aware of what was happening, I had become so wrapped up in newspaper work that I couldn't possibly escape from it. At any rate, I passed up the job and came East to do post-graduate work at Princeton for a Doctor's degree, some special work under Corwin, who had been hired to succeed Woodrow Wilson. A few weeks after I entered Princeton, President Hibben invited me to join the faculty, which I did for two years while I took my graduate work."

Change of scene and occupation was as necessary to his soul as food to his body. Lowell Thomas began his long career of exploration in 1916, interspersing his teaching and studying by organizing two expeditions to Alaska. He at once chose a land where men were in pursuit of the yellow metal, like the men he had known in his boyhood whose tales had woven themselves into his childhood dreams. When he returned to the United States after these expeditions, he was able to impart much of his own enthusiasm for the romantic way of life to the audiences that came to hear his lectures and early travelogues.

Lives of famous men reveal one startling consistency. The separate incidents are like the pieces of a picture puzzle. Each bears its proper relationship to the finished picture, revealing one continuous theme. Often we are told by a great man that he has always known that he has been picked out to do a special job, and that he has been impelled to follow his destiny. Such a man seems to have an inner awareness of his gift and of its responsibilities. By this knowledge, he is moved to select certain experiences and to reject all those that are extraneous to the main theme of his life. And so Lowell Thomas, throughout his kaleidoscopic career, selected that particular combination of opportunities which served to prepare him for the pursuits by which he was presently to distinguish himself.

Franklin K. Lane, Secretary of State in President Wilson's Cabinet in 1917, heard Thomas lecture. He noted that the young man was not only a capable raconteur but an accurate observer and interpreter of life in foreign lands. When the President wanted a pictorial record of the First World War, Lowell Thomas was mentioned by Lane for the position of Chief of the Civilian Mission. Thus in 1917, at the age of twenty-five, young Thomas was sent to Europe with a staff of camera men to gather the historical data for chronicling the World War right at the scene of battle.

After he had covered the line of trenches in France, Thomas found himself in Italy recording the struggle against the Austro-German armies. He took the cue for his next move from a placard stuck in a sandbag. It was a bulletin from Rome, telling about General Allenby's projected drive against the Turks in Palestine. A campaign in the Holy Land! This would provide vivid new scenes for his battery of cameras. Lowell Thomas maneuvered the cumbersome transfer with all his equipment, and arrived to add his tale to history's spectacular tales of the conquests of Jerusalem.

"It was there in Palestine that I had the break of my life," he records. "I happened upon that amazing phenomenon, Lawrence of Arabia." Perhaps you have read his *Boy's Life* of *Colonel Lawrence* or his *Lawrence of Arabia*. The latter he was persuaded to write in 1925, after he had spent three years lecturing the world over on the fantastic character of this English student who defeated the Turks. In this book, Thomas tells how, as he was walking in

Jerusalem shortly after his arrival, he saw a group of Arabians dressed in immaculate and stately robes, like the desert lords he had read of in the tales of the *Arabian Nights*. But he remarked that one among them was without a beard, and had blue eyes. He knew that every Arab, to be considered a grown man, wears a beard, and that they all have brown eyes. He went to the Military Governor of Jerusalem and inquired about the beardless one. The Governor introduced him to Colonel Lawrence himself. The Colonel, as everyone now knows, was a quiet, introspective man with far more reserve than could be attributed merely to his English origin. Only the ardent curiosity and dogged persistence of an experienced news gatherer such as Thomas could have pierced the impersonal exterior of Lawrence and emerged out of the Arabian desert with the full story intact. From the Governor and from Lawrence himself Thomas received permission to accompany the latter in order that he might record the story of the revolt at first hand. Lawrence was uniting the desert Arabian tribes against the onslaught of the Turks, a feat heretofore considered impossible. There was that indefinable magnetism in the man's personality that won the confidence and the adherence of each individual tribe. The story of his successful leadership was gathered for posterity by our own skillful American reporter.

When Thomas returned to the United States, he told this story to a large public audience in New York. He was advised to tell it in the Covent Garden Opera House in London—a fantastic idea, but it caught fire. There he presented it night after night to an audience that, in their hilarious appreciation, belied all traditional tales regarding the natural reserve of Englishmen. The fact that an American had come to tell them about the brilliant campaign waged by an Englishman little known to themselves seemed to make Lawrence's feat all the more worthy of acclaim. It is one thing for an Englishman to tell another, "We're good," but when an American travels across the ocean to tell them how good they are, that's news! Thomas soon found himself launched on a long tour of the British Empire, telling the story of Lawrence the world over. It took him as far as Australasia, India, and Malaya. He accompanied the Prince of Wales through India, and was invited to the courts of the great Maharajahs. Facilities were accorded him for an expedition into the wilds of Malaya and Upper Burma, and, to top it all, an invitation came from the Government of Kabul to visit the forbidden land of Afghanistan. This led to an exciting six months through Waziristan, the wild Khyber Pass, and the fierce land of the Afghans, where Thomas was entertained by King Amanullah in his palace in Kabul.

After his success with Lawrence, Thomas continued to travel and to write about adventures he encountered throughout the world. *Pageant of Adventure*, one of his latest books, is a selection of tales sifted out of the long years of travel, some of them chosen for the very reason that they had happened so unexpectedly to ordinary people in ordinary places. He traveled among the Pygmy tribes of the East and recorded their strange customs. He made motion pictures of a dying race of aborigines in Australia. He took his wife on a twenty-five-thousand-mile flying trip and visited twenty-eight countries. His journey through Afghanistan inspired him to write *Adventures in Afghanistan for Boys*.

These many years of writing and speaking gave Thomas a fluency of delivery that led to his receiving important radio assignments. What he refers to as his father's "hobby" for developing and fostering the art of speaking bore ripe fruit all through his life. From the very beginning, Lowell's voice was distinguished, and today it has an added quality. It is lifted slightly by humor, a humor muted so as not to destroy the serious import of his words as he gives his fifteen-minute radio digest of the world's happenings of the day. He enters the studio fifteen seconds before he starts to talk, holding in his hand the script he has been preparing up to the very last minute, with its interpolations of "latest news bulletins." As he seats himself before the microphone, he looks calm and rested, and proceeds with a precision that would be almost mechanical if it were not for the quality of natural warmth that is characteristically his.

One wonders where his curiosity will take this man next. It belongs to his pattern of living that he should maintain a constant search, like the gold miners of his boyhood who pursued the yellow metal. He himself is puzzled by this insatiable urge to be on the move, to peer into remote corners of the world for strange ways to photograph and record and then tell about.

The outstanding characteristic of Lowell Thomas' writing and speaking is its freedom from bias or judgment. "When you've been all around and seen all sorts of people, you get so you don't impose your critical faculty on humanity any more. I don't know just why." He appears, as he tries to explain his attitude, to be still the boy listening to adventure stories. Boys enthralled by such tales do not subject people's experiences to analysis and criticism;

they seem to take it for granted that a network of motives and unavoidable circumstances will cause men to act as they do. With Thomas, it is no mere studied indifference imposed by his profession as a radio news commentator. Rather it is that he likes people, that all kinds of people fascinate him. Color, race, and creed are factors inherent in a man's story, and as such do not influence Thomas in his relationships with people. He is not required to submit a script to his sponsors, yet his broadcast is rarely colored by propaganda of any kind. Occasionally, there may be an overemphasis or some humorous interpolation that seems to convey the merest shade of criticism. But never does he attack people; nor does he grind political axes.

In the past few years, Thomas' writing has shown him to be more than a teller of tales. In *Stand Fast for Freedom*, which he wrote in collaboration with Berton Braley, he turns the spotlight on world history and picks out the events, throughout the ages, that have woven the fabric of our American democracy today. It is a series of historical sketches showing how man has had to fight in order to evolve the "American Way," which so many of us take for granted. He ends with an exhortation to young boys and girls to safeguard those liberties for which men have struggled for centuries:

"If you guard this wealth of freedom with the same spirit of courage, faith, and devotion that moved Stephen Langton and John Hampden, that inspired Washington and Franklin and all the other founders of this republic, that held Lincoln steady on his course, the American Bill of Rights will remain a fortress of liberty that no power of treachery, terror, or tyranny can conquer."

In 1937, at the time of the greatest American flood, Thomas set out to write the story of this single catastrophe. But this incited his curiosity about all floods, and finally culminated in *Hungry Waters*, in which he tells the stories of the great floods of history.   Here he poses many questions:

"Why do these floods happen? Why are they becoming worse? We find ourselves plunged into the details of the lumber business, deforestation and reforestation, soil erosion and sound methods of husbandry. . . . Will some precautions be taken before another more devastating flood has swept down from the watersheds?"

In the role of parent, Thomas reveals wisdom and ability. He has a son who is evidently not going to be left out of the running in this hunt for adventure. Lowell Thomas, Jr., made a thirty-five-thousand-mile journey around Cape Horn to explore those waters when he was only fifteen. At seventeen, he went with a mountaineering expedition in Alaska, doing a man's work on the trip. The following summer he worked as a day laborer on a construction gang, the only white man in a crew made up entirely of colored men. The only instant during our interview that Lowell Thomas showed any pride at all over his lifework was when he told about this particular job of his son's.

Thomas likes music, preferably orchestral music. During the short week ends that he spends in his home in the country he is a sportsman. He has a fine horse that he trained from an unmanageable outlaw.   He has also organized a local softball team, called "The Nine Old Men." He allows himself one cigar a day in his rare moments of relaxation. A hard worker, he looks amazingly fit and unruffled. His secretary says that it is nothing for her to take dictation with a pencil in one hand and a sandwich in the other when they are out on a trip. Thomas dictates in taxicabs, standing on curbs. He appears to be saving himself for the fray of his work as he moves about with a sureness and calm born of many years of self-discipline.

The qualities that are responsible for Lowell Thomas' success are his intense curiosity, his love of action and adventure even in face of danger, his tolerance of and liking for people, and his rare ability to detect the knock of opportunity whenever and wherever it strikes.

All the World His Stage

Norman Bel Geddes

THERE WAS A BAD BUSINESS PANIC IN 1907, depression bore down upon the whole United States for several years thereafter. But by 1909 "Zedsky, the Boy Magician" was doing all right for a lad of sixteen, touring the small towns of Ohio with his bag of tricks. He quickly outgrew sleight-of-hand as a means of stunning his public, and contracted with the Gus Sun Circuit that same summer to appear as "Bob Blake, Eccentric Comedian." The first performance in Byesville, Ohio, was a flop. The thundering round of applause he expected failed to materialize, and Norman Bel Geddes retired as an actor. It was his second flop. The previous year, while delivering groceries at his grandfather's store, he organized the Empire Stock Company, a wagon troupe that disbanded after a single show.

Norman went back to school that fall, to the ninth grade, but not for long. He liked to sketch. He had been drawing funny pictures and painting ever since he was nine years old, when he built a theater in a neighbor's barn and painted the scenery for the productions on brown wrapping paper. During school recess one day, he faced a whole row of blackboards, washed clean and irresistible. While the other fellows were scrambling around working off steam, he grabbed a piece of chalk and quickly began to release his own pent-up energies by drawing four

25

gorgeous caricatures—one of the principal and three more
of the faculty. He was caught red-handed by his teacher,
who had him expelled from the halls of learning.

Geddes told me this story in an expansive mood. He
is in his forties now, but remembers the incident vividly.
Interviewers and reporters, writing about America's first
and greatest industrial designer, like to tell that incident
as a big joke, but to him it is still no laughing matter.

I was relieved to find myself seated beside Mr. Geddes,
listening to his genial voice reviewing his boyhood, for he
is a busy man if ever there was one. In his offices in Radio
City, some seventy-five technical assistants spend their day
sorting and trimming up the ideas for industrialists that
come tumbling out of his fertile brain, so that it was
quite an achievement for me to have secured an appointment after several encounters with his affable but ever-
present public relations representative.

I sat on the sofa in the modern reception room and
studied the photographs. They were "blow-ups" of Mr.
Geddes' designs, many of which I had already seen in the
flesh. There were photos of the General Motors World's
Fair Exhibit, with its Futurama. That project was investigated by the greatest number of people ever gathered to
view a single exhibit. It was a model that envisaged America in 1960. The most popular part was the express motor-
way linking all sections of the country. People stood in a
line twelve deep and half a mile long at the World's Fair
waiting to get into the Futurama. Once inside, they were
seated in cushioned parlor-car chairs that crept along on
a ramp, while a recorded voice described the sights as
they unfolded before their eyes.   It was not only an
imaginatively stimulating experience created out of the

ferment of one man's genius; it was a swell place to sit down. Lulled by the Voice of Tomorrow, one glided through this magical element.

More than half the World's Fair visitors went back to their home towns goggle-eyed at what can still be done to make civilization bearable. They learned that cities, far from being too crowded, could be packed with three and four times as many people, and still provide more space for gardens and fresh air than they now have. The buildings could be built much higher. Today's skyscrapers in that new world would look like little posts. City streets would be on two levels—one for pedestrians, one for autos. Most of our national highways, Geddes reminds us, were laid out by bison, and a good many of our city streets were planned by cows. That's why traffic in the middle of a big city can't go beyond an average of six miles an hour, whereas in the horse-and-buggy days folks could whiz through town at a speed of eleven miles. Change would be comparatively easy. All that needs to be done is to impress upon people that such change is feasible, which is what the Futurama attempted to do.

Other "blow-ups" and exhibits in this reception room tell about streamlining. There is a model of a motorcar built to ride more comfortably than any on the road today. If they thought the public was ready for it, manufacturers could commission Geddes to design a motorcar that so reduced the wind resistance that it would double its present speed and halve its present gas consumption. It would have the motor in the back, and look like a teardrop gliding on its side. Airplane fusillages are now designed in that shape. Geddes has recognized that streamlining is a science in itself. It is a concern of mathemati-

cians, physicists, and engineers. "The study of the effect
of form on air resistance began with Sir Isaac Newton in
1686," Geddes has written. "The weaning of public taste
from its illogical prejudices is paving the way. . . ." Aero-
dynamics holds the clue to the great innovations pred-
icated by Geddes to receive their fruition in the present
century.

In glass cases in the reception room are models of radios
in cabinets as simple and serviceable as human ingenuity
can devise. Photographs show the original of today's model
stove, designed by Geddes in 1929. It revolutionized the
domestic kitchen field. All its edges are round, and there
are no dust-catching grooves. It looks pleasant and invit-
ing to a woman who likes to cook. Other pictures show
bits of theater-stage settings, such as the fascinating one of
the play *Dead End*, where slum kids play at the river's end
against the wall of the garden apartment house of the
city's "swells," the whole thing raised to a pitch by clever
and original lighting.

While I waited in the reception room, Geddes' assistants—busy, interesting-looking men—kept rushing in and
out, interviewing visitors who had hoped to see Geddes.
I felt greedy and apprehensive about the promised appointment. Here were all these important-looking men
rolling up their blueprints and bidding the technical assistants a reluctant goodbye, while I stayed on, prodding
to be squeezed in on this busy man's program.

At last I was called. I had time to notice the doorknobs,
each a big handful, with a squared-off edge for you to get
a good grip on as it is turned. I stepped into a room about
thirty feet long, so scantily furnished that all I was conscious of was a table and one man in profile. The man

looked like a laborer from the waist up and like an apprentice in a clerical office from the waist down. I don't know what gives Norman Bel Geddes that remarkable development of head. chest, and shoulders. He is of only average height, but from his pictures, I had expected to see a six-footer. He has a large head and a wide jaw that you notice pleasantly when he breaks into an occasional chuckle. The pupils of his eyes burn so darkly that I was unable to tell what color his eyes were. His manner was friendly. He addressed me with an air of being utterly natural, which I found more pleasing than the attitude of gallantry some older men assume.

We sat down at the big table. The table was just a block of wood about five feet long, and looked worn and cozy. It was very low, and I'll bet it is used for a footrest. I doffed my coat because the room, in spite of its size, seemed comfortably warm. I realized at once that the atmosphere of warmth came from the soft gleam of the ceiling lights that were inserted in glass discs flush with the ceiling. No curtains at the windows. Not a single ornament visible anywhere. Not even a picture on the walls. Instantly I was struck by what Geddes had done with his office. He had designed it by applying exactly the same principle he used in designing everything else. As in his stage setting, instead of "props," he used lighting and shade to create atmosphere.

Geddes was the first to use this principle in the theater. His fame dates back twenty years, to the time when he was a producer and presented plays in his own novel scenic garb. He never liked to clutter a stage with scenery. "Pauses merely to change scenes are intolerable and inexcusable," he said. "The audience is not to be conscious of any scenery or background other than the mood in which the characters of this particular play should move." He used to change scenes simply by having the actors appear in another set on the stage and by shifting the light. In *Hamlet*, he planned a platform that became in turn a throne dais, a grave, and a players' stage. An aperture between two towering blocks became now a dark corridor, now an empty abyss separating Hamlet from the supernatural world. What need for a man of such economical inventiveness to decorate his own office? There was not a single diversion to break through the current of our conversation.

Ruminating over his boyhood disgrace, Geddes explained why it had been especially serious for such a thing to have happened in his family:

"You see, my mother was on the faculty in that school. My father was dead, and she worked as a music supervisor. It was her own idea, now quite an accepted procedure in the public schools. With a good musical education, she went to the University of Michigan and developed the teaching of music in public schools. She sold the schools the idea of hiring a music supervisor who would go from room to room and school to school, and take on the music assignments in each school in a town. That was a step in advance of the current practice, whereby each teacher attempted to handle the subject of music in her own class, without any special training or talent. My mother was trying out her plan in our school just at the time they expelled me. I felt awful about it. But mother was an understanding person; she didn't lay it on.

Then a funny thing happened. James Donahey, the cartoonist for the *Cleveland Plain Dealer*, heard about the incident. The story got to him through someone who knew of his own experience. Exactly ten years before my downfall, that cartoonist had been expelled from the same school, by the same teacher, and for the same reason! He wrote me a letter offering to help me if I would go to see him. I did, and he got me into the Cleveland School of Art. But I wasn't happy there, and left after three months."

This happened in 1912. Geddes then tried the Chicago Art Institute. After seven weeks at the new school, he met Hendrik Lund, the Norwegian painter, who took an interest in him and advised him to give up art schools and go his own way. At the same time, he got a job for the Barnes Crosby Company, an advertising illustration firm, lettering numbers on Sears Roebuck fashion plates for their catalogue at three dollars a week. He gave that up in six weeks, and in 1914 left Chicago for Detroit. Here he was not given a job, but was allowed to compete with other designers of an advertising firm in Detroit. Six months later, he became their art director. Geddes was then twenty-one. Things began to look up. The Barnes Crosby Company opened a Detroit branch. Without recognizing the youth they had let slip at a three-dollar salary less than a year before, they asked him to come back as manager of their Detroit branch for a hundred and twenty-five dollars and five per cent commission.

While on this job, Geddes published a thirty-two-page monthly magazine called *Inwhich* ("In which I say what I think"), doing the editing, illustrating, and printing himself. That lasted two years. At the same time, he wrote a play about the American Indian called *Thunderbird*, and sold it to a Los Angeles theater company. His continued broad interest in various subjects irritated his em-

ployers, and they demanded that he either relinquish his
other interests or resign from their firm. He chose to resign, and went to Los Angeles, where his play was to be
produced. He now busied himself at once with designing
theatrical productions of plays by such writers as D. H.
Lawrence, W. B. Yeats, Arthur Schnitzler, and Zoe Atkins.
Those were wonderful days, free for experimentation in
a beloved field. It was Geddes who first introduced spot
lamps, today in universal use, as the sole means of stage
lighting.

Geddes was twenty-three when his first child was born,
and the Universal Film Company lured him into the
movie field. That proved a fiasco for him. He described
that experience ruefully:

"I signed up with the Universal Film Company, Los
Angeles, to produce *Nathan Hale*, a patriotic short that I
had written. Those were the silent-picture days, and this
picture was an innovation in that there was not a single
title until the very last scene, which showed Nathan Hale
going to his death. Then the screen flashed Hale's famous
line: 'My only regret is that I have but one life to give
for my country.' Coming at the end of twenty minutes
of sheer pantomime, it was an effective closing. We were
at war at the time.

"I couldn't get used to the movie method of using the
sun in place of electrical illumination. In those days, they
shot their scenes out of doors, and reflected the sun with
large mirrors in such a way as to outdo the sun's caprices.
The slow film of that time was unpredictable when I tried
to introduce artificial lighting. Besides that, something
sinister happened to make me dislike the movie industry
even more. I had just bought a house and filled it with

new furniture when the rainy season came on. As we sat in the living room of our new house, I suddenly found myself getting damp all over. They built such fragile homes for the transient crowd out there that the roofs couldn't withstand even the first rain. So, disgusted with the house and discouraged by the methods used by the movie industry, I quit the job after six weeks, in spite of a two-year contract and the fact that I had just five dollars to cushion the blow when I went home to my wife and baby and reported what I had done."

This led to the story of his first days in New York. I had heard a little about that, and asked: "Wasn't Otto Kahn the man who gave you a real start in New York? I read that you sent him a two-page telegram from Los Angeles, and he answered it by telegraphing you four hundred dollars the same day. Do you have the words of that telegram?"

"No, I don't have a copy, but Mr. Kahn had the original telegram framed. I was surprised when I came into his office a few years ago and saw it above his desk. I asked him why. He said: 'That telegram represents one of the best investments I have ever made.' "

"What were the conditions that came with that donation?" I wanted to know.

"Absolutely none. That was the part I couldn't understand. But I paid it all back within a year. I was barely twenty-five and at the end of a career, the movie career. When I quit the Universal Film Company, I went out in the park and sat down on a bench. A man alongside of me had been reading a magazine. He got up, letting it slip to the ground. My eyes passed listlessly over the headings of the articles, as the wind turned the pages slowly. Sud-

denly, I was arrested by the headline: 'Millionaires Should
Help Young Artists.' I stuck my foot out and held that
place in the magazine. It was the *Literary Digest*. I picked
it up and read the article. It was an interview with Otto
Kahn. I spent most of the last five dollars on a telegram,
telling him what I had done and asking him to lend me
enough money to go to New York and look for a job as a
stage designer. He telegraphed me four hundred dollars
the same day.

"I arrived in New York with a big wooden box full of
designs for stage sets and costumes. The box was too heavy
to be carried. I wouldn't spend good money on a cab, so
I pushed that box the size of a small trunk from the express station across town to Mr. Kahn's office on Pine
Street. I arrived as he was about to leave for the week
end. He refused to see me or the work I had brought to
show him. He was glad he had been able to help me; now
that I had my check and was in New York I was on my
own. But I kept after his secretary and finally got in.

"Kahn was a short fellow, and seemed cold as ice. He
looked holes through me and scared the gizzards out of
me. I couldn't believe his not wanting to see my drawings. He wanted no proof that his money had been well
invested. Then, reacting to my apparent disappointment,
he softened. He invited me to join him at breakfast
Tuesday morning, when he returned to the city; he would
look at my stuff then. That interview led to an introduction to Gatti Casazza at the Metropolitan Opera House.
That afternoon, I was engaged to design my first production in New York—sets for several operas."

Geddes began at once to demonstrate the validity of his
theory that the stage designer must have the point of view

of the director. Every detail of the stage—scenery, lighting,
and costumes—must be the organic outgrowth of the
author's action.   His work was so original that it immediately got the attention of theatrical producers in the
metropolis. Each successful play led to a flock of new assignments to design scenery, costumes, and lighting for
theatrical productions.

Within three years, Geddes was the busiest designer in
New York. At the same time, he drew assignments to paint
portraits of Caruso, Galli-Curci, Cavalieri, and other
musical and acting celebrities. He had had experiences
in both these fields in his late adolescence and early twenties in the West. He had exhibited his paintings for the
first time as a youngster the same year that he managed
a laundry agency to help support the family.

Norman Bel Geddes has shown as much genius in knowing when to quit a venture as in knowing upon what to
focus his energies.   He places great faith in his own
"hunches." He might have agonized over charcoal drawings of plaster models in the art school, but he quit that.
He might have accepted the ultimatum of the Detroit firm
and given up the theater, but he didn't. He might have
struggled to confine his own imaginative genius to the
limited possibilities of the movie field of that day, but he
left the movies and his brand-new, rained-in house, and
came to New York imploring the help of a stranger. About
these courageous decisions, which worked out successfully,
he comments:

"Some things in life you know without knowing how
you know them. You know that there is a certain thing
you can do if you want to and if you are not afraid of
the unexpected. Every important step I have ever taken

has come about as the result of some spontaneous inner conviction. Listen to your own inner convictions. Experiment. You may hear something unexpected that is worth while."

One day Geddes was walking down Fifth Avenue in New York and looking into shop windows when a new conviction stopped him dead. Why must window displays be treated in so dull a fashion? Why couldn't a big store window be fixed up like a stage, the object suggesting the action with which the merchandise will eventually be associated? As these thoughts ran through his mind, he found himself staring critically at the old-fashioned display window of one store, which was no different from any other display window of the day. He prepared a five-page letter embodying his ideas to the president of the store. Three months later, New York got its first introduction to a new type of window display that is now standard all over the country. That conviction and the venture to which it led proved to be a significant training ground, for it was the beginning of the momentous change in Geddes' career.

There now followed two years of handling consumer goods—clothes, furnishings, perfumes, interior decorations. Geddes grew more and more interested. He kept getting new ideas for improving merchandise, making it more attractive, more serviceable, more economical to manufacture. The desire to experiment made him restive. He had another hunch. He went from window display to the designing of consumer goods.

At twenty-seven, Geddes gave vent to a spirit that permitted his true genius to flourish. His offices became an experimental station. All the world's goods became sud-

denly alive as ideas for improving them bubbled forth
from his brain. It was incredible to him that in the field
of industrial production no thorough critical review was
being made of the new consumer goods. After launching
some clever modern device, such as an electric refrigerator,
a manufacturer was content to turn out exact replicas of
the original in hundreds of thousands. Geddes was not
content. He bought three refrigerators and a dozen ther-
mometers. He hung them all over the inside of the refrigerators, and found that the temperatures varied greatly
at different levels of the interior. He redesigned the shelves
to fit the foods that belonged on each according to their
temperature requirements.

He studied motorcars, realizing the waste caused by the
chunky shape of the car as it battled the wind it created
in stubborn waves around its clumsy corners. That started
him on the whole principle of "streamlining." This principle he applied to ships, to trains, to anything that moved.
A few old designers had made half-hearted concessions, but
Geddes' absorption with these problems was considered
even by his friends as "an eccentric gesture." At last, the
eyes of the biggest manufacturers turned furtively toward
drawings of his marvelous new designs. Gradually, although they hardly dared risk the open market, blaming
a skeptical and laggard public, they sought his advice on
every type of goods.

Geddes is out of the theater now, caught up in the dramatic career of designing for a greater stage—the world of
tomorrow. Many of his ideas are as far ahead of reality as
were those of Jules Verne and Leonardo da Vinci, but he
appears to be able to keep both feet on the ground whenever the occasion requires it. When you read about the

kind of city he envisions, you find your blood pressure
mounting. In his book *Horizons*, his awareness of our
present direction and his predictions read like an oracle:

"We enter a new era. Are we ready for the changs
that are coming? . . . It happens that the United States
has seized upon more of the fruits of industrialism than
any other nation. We have gone farther and more swiftly
than any other. To what end? Not the least tendency is
the searching and brooding uncertainty, the quest for basic
truths which characterize the present day. Never before,
in an economic crisis, has there been such an aroused con-
sciousness on the part of the community at large and
within industry itself. Complacency has vanished. A new
horizon appears. A horizon that will inspire the next
phase in the evolution of the age."

That was in 1932. While we were in the doldrums of
a depression, Norman Bel Geddes was busy nursing a
vision. A decade later, with a populace tense over a new
world war, he has kept his staff busy with the constructive
details for life as he conceives of it in 1945 and 1950.
He employs seventy-five assistants who are experts in every
phase of creative design—color, line, functionalism, mer-
chandising, engineering, and manufacturing. He himself
devotes three fourths of his time to production planning
for the post-war period. According to him:

"Business has never been better in our field. We find
that businessmen all over the country are busy preparing
for the new era following an Allied victory. They expect
to introduce materials in harmony with changed methods
of living. The habits acquired during wartime, making
the most sensible use of goods to conserve materials needed
in conflict, are making the public more receptive to the

thousands of improved products that businessmen have
been engaged upon."

He quoted from a manuscript he was then preparing
for publication:

"Wars accelerate technological progress because of the
new materials, new inventions, and new manufacturing
methods developed. . . . Limitations pave the way for sub-
stitutes and replacements.

"It is the industrial designer who is given the task of
anticipating the trend and character of the product development of the future."

Everything his eye falls upon becomes a challenge to his
creative genius. Being told that a thing cannot be done
is his cue for proceeding to do it. That has ever been his
mode of progress.

Even as a parent, Geddes seems to have some arresting
ideas. His two daughters have each maintained their own
apartments in the city since they were sixteen. They submit a weekly statement of their expenditures to their
father, and get their next week's allowance.

"What happens if they've overspent their allowance?"
I was skeptical.

"They would have to make it up. But they are very
good in this respect. They never do, that's all."

If you find your mind refusing to accept this method of
rearing daughters, remember that Geddes' startling ideas,
both in the theater and in industrial production, have
stunned the conventional public for the past twenty years.
He has been right in his conceptions most of the time.
We who live and think in grooves are indebted to him for
his audacity. His daughters, too, seem to have thrived well
on his experimentation. Joan—"she's the intellectual"—

the elder, was busy writing radio scripts for an agency at the time Geddes told me of his career. Barbara—"she's more like me"—was then nineteen, and playing the leading part in the road-company production of *Junior Miss*. Geddes tries to protect them from the unfortunate effects of having a parent whose name is in the public eye. Perhaps that is one reason why he has allowed them to set up independent dwellings.

Norman Bel Geddes has gone a long way since he was expelled from school and worked as bellboy on a steamer, where he met the magician who touched off his early ambition to force an audience to wake up and listen. Michigan, Syracuse, and Adrian have given him honorary degrees, which makes up for that boyhood blight. The world has voted him many high honors, not only because his inventive and prophetic genius has resulted in the production of so many creature comforts, but because of his example of courage, daring, and confidence, without which he might still be painting labels or decorating department-store windows, earning a "safe" income at some nine-to-five job instead of taking big chances and working twice as many hours with ten times the results for himself and for posterity.

Heroine in Shorts

ALICE MARBLE

NOW THERE'S A GIRL who has everything. If the tennis
champion had never played a game in her life,
Alice Marble would nevertheless have been included in
one of those lists that organizations draw up annually of
famous people. First of all, she is good to look at, with
her golden crown of hair cut in the latest vagabond style,
her large green-tinted eyes with the slightly overhanging
lids, her pert nose, and her husky, endearing voice. She
speaks like a delighted child, breaking often into a wide,
warm smile that makes one cheek dimple. She has a crisp,
tingling quality. But I could go on and on about her
piquant personality, and there are many other things
about her worth telling.

Alice Marble was twenty-seven at the time of our interview, and a serious, hard-working young woman. She
was devoting long hours at her office desk, keeping two
secretaries busy. She had to travel often to Washington to
confer with government big-wigs. She attended big dinners at which photographers loved to snap her sitting
demurely beside the speakers and officials who have been
running the civilian defense show. Her photogenic face
had brightened the pages of many a news story and magazine article devoted to the physical fitness program for
defense. She addresses groups and women's clubs. She
had been writing, giving interviews, and listening to civic

41

group leaders for their ideas. In the role of Director of
Civilian Defense in Charge of National Physical Fitness
for Women, she was receiving one dollar a year from the
Government. It was a big job, sixteen hours a day sometimes. Besides her work, she was responsible for just being
what she is, for the public expected her to exemplify that
physical well-being that she had been engaged to promote.
She responded generously to questions about her personal
life, if the information was to be used in the national physical fitness cause, and I, too, found her more than
co-operative.

"What do you do, Miss Marble, when you're physically
exhausted?" was one of the questions I asked her. Her face
became suddenly earnest in a characteristic change of expression as swift as her court play. She treated my question and her answer to it as part of her government assignment to make good health popular in the United States.

"I take a bath, get into fresh, clean clothes, and go out
for a long, brisk walk." Then she broke into a smile and
added, "And sometimes I play tennis."

"Don't you ever lie down when you're tired?"

"No, I can't do that in the daytime somehow. But I
do find reading relaxing."

She believes that most of us need more, rather than less,
exercise when we're tired. She acquired that belief from
her mother's example when she was a very young child.

"My mother, although she married when she was thirty-
four, had five children; so you can imagine she was no
young woman when I was a little girl, for I was the fifth.
Mother had a big household to direct and no end of
housework all day. But every evening we had our supper
at five, and then she would take the whole family out to

the Golden Gate Park in San Francisco and play games
with us. Mother actually participated in active sports with
my brothers and myself; she said it rested her. Then we'd
all walk home and be in bed by eight o'clock. Even when
I was in high school, that routine continued, with the
eight-o'clock bedtime."

Mrs. Marble set the example also of dual achievement
that Alice has followed. The father died in an automobile
accident when Alice was only six, placing the entire parental burden on the mother. He had been a cattle rancher
in Plumas County, California, where he eked out a rather
meager income doing lumbering and other seasonal work
in the county and farming his own land for the family's
food. When he died, the two older boys went to work to
support the large family, but mother and the five children
continued to spend their leisure hours together in active
play.

It was after the father's death that the family moved to
San Francisco. They lived close by the athletic courts of
the Golden Gate Park. Here Alice served a long apprenticeship for her world-renowned racquet playing. Tennis
was not her first love, however. That she considered a
"sissy" game, devoting herself to baseball with her three
brothers. "You know," she explained, "ball games for us
kids were such an inexpensive hobby. We could have fun
just reading the papers and talking about our national
heroes. We were poor, so naturally we picked a hobby
that was cheap." Her brothers allowed her to play with
them because she was a good sport and learned to swat a
ball as vigorously as any boy. In describing her tennis
playing, Miss Marble is charmingly modest, but her eyes
still light up with pride as she says, "I can throw a baseball

today as fast as any man." When she won the Associated
Press Poll of 1939 as the most outstanding woman athlete
in the country, it was said that her sheer power of stroke
was supreme in female tennis playing. The fellows who
used to play with her in Golden Gate Park must have enjoyed reading that, for they knew how she had acquired it.

Miss Marble won honorable mention even a year before
the Associated Press Poll as one of the ten most outstanding women in America. She was then twenty-five, and was
selected by American Women. In their *Who's Who,* she
reports that her "hobby" is tennis. She actually means it.
Her cheek dimples every time she mentions the game. No
matter how many details pile up in reference to her many
jobs, she sweeps through them with great efficiency and
makes sure to save room on her heavy schedule for her
daily tennis practice. "Sometimes after a day's work I am
so tired as I get ready to play," she confessed in one of
her addresses, "that I don't feel much like it, but as soon
as I start to play I forget everything and just enjoy it."

Not until she was fifteen did Miss Marble lend an ear
to her brothers who had been urging her to switch from
baseball to tennis. By presenting her with a tennis racquet
one day, they indicated tactfully that she was getting too
grown up to rough and tumble with them on the baseball
field. She took the hint and, without enthusiasm, wandered
over to the municipal courts, lugging the new racquet.
There a tennis tournament was in process of being organized. Somehow she found herself signed up for the competition. Of the fifteen courts to be used, twelve were wet
when the girls went out to play, so she and the other contestants dragged blankets across them until they dried out.
She tells how, by that little preparatory exercise, she found

her interest in the game warming up surprisingly. Of course, she was out at the very beginning of the play. Much chagrined at this ham performance, she became bent on making a better showing. Having discovered that tennis was not an easy game, she regarded it more respectfully, and from that time on, it was tennis in every leisure moment for Alice.

Her new hobby was a bit more expensive, for it meant buying racquets and balls and tennis shoes—all on a seventy-five-cent-a-week allowance. Miss Marble recalled that when she won the Pacific Coast Junior and Women's Championship, she was playing with a borrowed racquet. "It was a little on the dead side and weighed fifteen ounces—like playing with a screen door." Courts were free, thank goodness. The hitch was that you had to be good to get a chance to do a decent amount of playing, because, when you applied for a court, you were put on a list. If you had finished and lost your first set, you were placed at the bottom of the list and had to wait two hours to play again. If you won, you stayed on the court and took on the next person on the list.

Many a time tomboy Alice was out after the first set in those early days. But long waits meant a chance to observe all kinds of players. It also meant volleying on the soft dirt in front of the clubhouse, or listening to words of wisdom about the game dropped from the lips of the big tennis players. One of these—a young fellow of whom Alice recalled with some feeling, "I was awfully fond of him at that time"—observing her powerful, masculine stroke, believed she had something worth cultivating. He knew Eleanor Tennant, a former national ranking tennis player and an excellent instructor, and asked her to come

down to the courts and watch the blonde tomboy play. Miss
Tennant was at once struck by the young high-school
girl's ability, and offered to give her lessons. From that
time to the present day, Miss Tennant has been "Teach" to
Alice, as she has been to many another ranking tennis player, including Bobby Riggs, twice national amateur champion.

The role of Miss Tennant deserves a big place in this
sketch, for it was her years of training, her steady faith in
her pupil, and her unwavering determination to make a
national champion out of Alice Marble that are in a great
measure responsible for the tennis player's fame in her
early twenties. "Teach" took Alice on at fifteen. At seventeen, she was already known in the Pacific Coast as a
"brilliant but erratic" player. She used to be greatly vexed
over her mistakes and cocky rather than confident over
her successes. She had to be taught poise and mental
balance as much as technique. Miss Marble never ceases
to add, when anyone tells of the training she received from
Miss Tennant, that she learned as much from her about
the correct mental attitude toward life as she did about
tennis. She learned that the will to win had to be there,
stronger and more enduring than the power of her fastest
stroke.

The importance of this factor was magnified by the fact
that Miss Marble was handicapped by two long and serious
illnesses during her career. In 1933, she collapsed at East-
hampton, Long Island, after playing a hundred and eight
games in a temperature of one hundred degrees. The doctors declared it was sunstroke, and she spent a winter under medical care. The very next year she went over with
five other girls to play in the international tournament in
Paris, and collapsed again. She returned in two weeks.

Miss Tennant was shocked when she met her pupil at the pier, being helped down the gangplank by two men. Neither one of them thought of giving up, but Miss Marble's illness was this time diagnosed as pleurisy. She spent six months in bed in a sanatorium. Her reflections on that period are illuminating:

"It was a most valuable period for me, although at the time I resented the dreadful waste of time away from my beloved tennis. I had leisure to think a lot and to read. I developed an attitude toward life in general that has stood me in good stead since. I became poignantly aware that good health is the most valuable of human possessions, and as such worth guarding with the utmost care. I didn't know it then, but the whole period of my illness was as important for my career as any other preparation I have had. Sounds funny to speak of illness as a fortunate circumstance, but it was really that."

After six months in bed, Miss Marble had to learn to walk again, at first only one block, then a thousand feet, and at last three miles a day. But her condition was still too poor for any serious tennis. She spent thousands of dollars and lost valuable time in search of a doctor who would cure her listlessness and give her some assurance that she would some day recover sufficiently to play. Five specialists said she was through with tennis. At last she found a doctor who, as he examined her, said:

"You are Alice Marble, the tennis player, aren't you?"

"I once was a tennis player," she replied, almost beaten.

"My dear girl, there is no reason to think you will not play tennis again. Your whole trouble comes from an anemic condition which I can take care of in two months' time."

He proved it at once. In two weeks her hemoglobin

count jumped from the dangerous low of 55 to the normal
of 88. She began to feel like moving about. The next
problem was to build up the unused muscles in her legs,
arms, shoulders, wrists, and diaphragm. She spent a month
doing back exercises. She jumped rope ten or fifteen
minutes every morning to strengthen the calves of her legs.
She took long, brisk walks daily. For her diaphragm she
took up singing. She has inherited a good voice from her
mother and loves to sing. This alone made her period of
illness worth while, for she so improved her voice that she
was able, in the winter of 1939, between tennis seasons, to
perform admirably as a supper club singer in the famous
Sert Room of the Waldorf Astoria. The experience was
important in that it added to her self-confidence, which
she needed in her tennis play. The relaxed attitude is
.1ecessary in all sports. "Besides," she says, "I felt that if
I could do well in something that was really new to me
then I did not have to fear for anything in tennis, the
game to which I was so accustomed." This, incidentally,
is one of the best arguments in favor of cultivating a
hobby.

Money was still scarce in the Marble family while Alice
was trying to recover her health. She worked toward the
latter part of this period as Miss Tennant's secretary. It
was a job she could do under her teacher's supervision
during the hours when she felt well, and it gave her an
opportunity to pay her way. With her mother's permission, she went to live with "Teach," so that the process
of re-training could be managed with the most economical
use of time and energy. Her diet was strictly prescribed
by the doctor who had successfully diagnosed her ailment.

Miss Marble does not like to discuss diet, preferring to

leave that subject to the nutrition experts, for she is aware that what is food for one man may be poison for another. Once, however, in an article, she did reveal a few fundamental food facts that were applied in her particular case. She had to go in for lots of rare beef, orange juice, milk, and green salads. She keeps her weight under control—about 130 pounds—and her height is five feet seven. "We all eat too much," she commented in that article, describing her lunch of a mixed vegetable salad and a glass of milk.

Other articles by Miss Marble followed. She has written for a number of magazines. Her style is direct, sincere, and soundly intelligent. She never had a college education. "Not that I wouldn't like to have gone to college, but I was giving so many hours to training that there was no time for anything else." She speaks as she writes, with the broad and understanding point of view of a properly educated person. Undoubtedly, her experience in travel and in meeting people add up to at least a B.A. achieved in the shade of sheltering elms around a college campus.

But to go back to the period of Miss Marble's convalescence. Perhaps the most dangerous part of this setback was the fear that the public would never get over thinking of the tennis player as a sickly has-been. When she was well again and ready to enter tennis tournaments, the officials refused to let her play. They were afraid to take the chance. At last, she prevailed upon several Eastern committeemen to consent to watch her play two hours a day for a full week in New York's hottest weather. She had learned by this time the trick of drinking two or three extra glasses of water a day with a large pinch of salt to replace the water and salt lost during active play. Finally the National Tennis Association gave its consent, and she entered the national tournament.

"The happiest moment of my life came," she declared, "when I won the last point of my match with Helen Jacobs, to be crowned Women's National Singles Champion of America." Imagine the thrill of that, coming directly upon a two years' struggle to win against an almost fatal illness and in defiance of a host of doctors who had declared she would never play tennis again. In spite of this triumph, she lived in mortal fear all that season that she might sometime sneeze or cough in the public's hearing. It would take nothing more than that to destroy the public's confidence in her health. Fortunately, all that she got was a blister on her foot. Since that year she continued to hang up records for her tournament play. Hers is an all-court game; she is as capable at the net as at the base line. She plays hard, smashing the ball, with a fast, American twist serve. She is supreme in overhead play, and all sports commentators refer to her powerful masculine stroke as the chief factor in her superiority over other women players.

"Do you think, Miss Marble," I asked her, "that women are as good in sports as men?"

She replied at once, "No, I don't. I think the female figure is against a woman in athletics. But even if this weren't so, there's a good reason why men do better today. Men have been in sports since the time of the ancient Greeks, whereas women have only been allowed to participate in this field to any degree for the past fifty or a hundred years. Perhaps in time their bodies will change, as generation after generation continues to be more athletic. When the time comes that a woman who is ath-

letic will no longer be regarded as the unusual type, when it will seem as natural for women as it now seems for men to be keenly interested in athletics, we'll start training girls to be active athletes. We'll not discourage them, as we do today, from taking part in 'tomboy' play when they're six, and ten, and twelve."

In 1939, Miss Marble was the first woman player to win in the same year the English and American women's singles, doubles, and mixed doubles championship. By the fall of 1940, she had won the national women's singles championship four times. Since then, she has had a busy and varied career. WNEW, an independent radio station in New York, needed a football reporter and hired her for fifteen-minute football analysis broadcasts twice a week. At the first broadcast, in her selection of winnings for the following day, she picked correctly thirty-one out of forty-five, and three others were ties. Skeptical but admiring masculine listeners grew respectful. She has also lectured at women's colleges, and *Who's Who* gives her a line as a dress designer of women's sports clothes.

Miss Marble's most important job at the time I talked with her was that of teaching the civilian female population of the country to keep physically fit. On this dollar-a-year government job, she appeared before women's clubs, colleges, church groups, and forums, helping to organize local groups devoted to the ideal of physical fitness. She is a strong advocate of physical exercise for women in their middle years, and for women who think they are "too tired." She observed in England, in 1939, that women of fifty and even sixty-five played tennis, took long bicycle trips and hikes, preparing themselves physically for men's jobs during wartime. Knowing that most women are bored with solo calisthenics, she advocates setting-up groups with free community instruction in sports and active games. Whenever she talks to a group, she takes into consideration the difficulties of that particular group for getting proper exercise in their environment and on their particular work schedules. I heard her address a girls' club in New York. The audience was made up mainly of office workers, living in the heart of this crowded city. Knowing how difficult and often expensive such sports as tennis or golf might prove for them, she gave them more practical suggestions for keeping fit. She stressed walks. She never forgets to stress brisk walking as an exercise. Then she described the advantages of dancing as an exercise, and of singing. Then she dwelt on the importance of posture. All the girls stuck out their chests. Miss Marble herself stands tall and proud. She looked regal on the platform this particular evening, wearing a silver-satin blouse and a cerise velvet, ankle-length skirt. Her face was earnest and serious, for she was talking about the subject that had been the most vital in her career. By the time that audience rose to leave the lecture hall, they were standing tall and feeling fresh and eager to practice her suggestions. I took the longest way home, and walked. Alice Marble sets that kind of example.

"What will you do about tennis next season?" I ventured, not sure whether it was fair to ask her to commit herself.

"I don't know, really. Of course, I'll always play tennis. But I don't know whether I'll continue as a professional tournament player or not."

That's Alice—honest, absorbed in what she is doing, persevering, and faithful. Even if tennis had not been her medium, her other qualities would have carried her far.

We Investigate the Investigator

SAMUEL UNTERMYER

A LITTLE GIRL OF FOUR, in her dainty frock, went trip-
ping one day through the Greek garden of her
great grandfather's estate in suburban New York. The
old man followed her slowly. She looked up at him and
said roguishly, "Let's dance."

"I can't," he shrugged. Samuel Untermyer, now past
eighty, a man who had always been able to give a superb
performance, was at last baffled by this chit.

"Oh, sure you can. Come on," she urged.

His keen old eyes swept the garden furtively. He
sidled over to his little companion and made, for him, a
cataclysmic admission. As a cross-examining attorney, he
was renowned for his resourcefulness, but this day he
bent down and whispered to the child.

"I don't know what to do."

"Come on," she commanded gently. "You can just do
anything. Like this," and she stretched out her arms,
shook her curls, and skipped in a circle. Soon the aged
tycoon of the legal profession, studying her movements
with surprise and delight, ventured a few feeble steps in
sheepish imitation.

Mrs. Irene Richter, who recounted this incident about
Samuel Untermyer, her father, commented, "And that
is about the only time I can remember that the spirit of a
child did not elude him. It was not until he was very

old that he really took the time to indulge in sentiment—
when he was very old and when he was very young."

Mrs. Richter is Samuel Untermyer's only daughter. He
had two sons, but Irene was the apple of her father's eye.
During the years of his greatest public achievement, when
he was conducting the investigations of monopolies, she
went with him daily to court. He "discovered" her in
her teens, intrigued by the half-mature mind of early
adolescence, and from that time on she traveled with him
often. When he was ill and worried about his eyesight,
she accompanied him on a round of visits to doctors in
Europe, comforting him in his fears and manufacturing
reassurances for his peace of mind. She was with him after
court appearances to absorb the shocks of his electric
temperament. His co-workers knew him as a tireless
worker and a most difficult man to pace, but his daughter
saw him as a man wracked and harassed by the vicissi-
tudes of his own genius, and extended the sympathy and
understanding that he so needed.

It was a warm, almost maternal greeting that she extended to me as I stood at her door one cold, rainy morning. She relieved me of my wet rubbers and dripping
umbrella, and I sank comfortably in a big armchair.

"To tell the truth," she apologized, "I don't really
know whether I have much to give you about my father
that you haven't already learned from others. You see,
he was a very busy, a very public man. But I'll try to
remember all I can about the things he used to tell me
of his childhood and youth."

Her eyes have the same gay twinkle that her father's
had. Samuel Untermyer used to disarm his witnesses with
it. His daughter possesses also his energy, mental alert-

ness, and fluidity of speech. She painted a vivid portrait of a hard man with an overdeveloped sense of self-discipline who expected his family to exercise the same stoic qualities in their daily conduct. "At heart, he was really a romanticist and a sentimentalist, but he had had to stifle that strain for the sake of his work until he no longer felt it. But all during the years when he was famous as a lawyer, he relied on the memory of emotions he once had experienced in his youth to play upon the emotions of the people he needed to influence in court."

Samuel Untermyer, crusader against the money trust, against Wall Street stock exchange abuses, against Nazi persecutions, against private ownership of public utilities, and against many similar injustices toward the little man, started in his early adolescence to play upon court audiences with an emotional power that he diverted to material uses for the remainder of his career. As a clerk in his brother's law offices, while still studying law at Columbia in his free hours, he was sent down to the New York Court of Appeals to argue cases. He was then seventeen. In those days, apparently the regulation that a man could not try a case until fully admitted to the Bar was not taken too literally, for Samuel Untermyer, "the Cantor with the beard," was allowed to appear eight times before he received his law degree, at twenty-one. He grew the beard to hide his youth and to counteract the effect of his not quite changed voice. Thus fantastically and ineffectively disguised, his youth only attracted more attention to his ability. He was just feeling his oats as an unadmitted attorney, egged on to furious efforts by the disparaging remark of Randolph Guggenheimer, his half-brother, to whom he was apprenticed. Randolph, who lived to acknowledge his mistake cheerfully, went to Samuel's mother one day and said, "Why don't you take that boy out of my office? He'll never make a good lawyer."

That was all he needed. The lad who had spent a carefree, placid boyhood without any driving hobbies or ambitions drew upon himself the responsibilities of adulthood in less than a year's time. He became an avid student of the law, although as a child he had been just an average pupil in the New York public schools. Eventually, he became a partner in the firm of Guggenheimer and Untermyer. When Maurice, his favorite brother, was admitted to the Bar, he also joined the firm. They employed in this law firm practically every relative in the entire family who did not put up an active resistance against it. This was engineered by Untermyer in a patriarchal manner.

Untermyer once said, exaggerating for the sake of making his point, that if a lawyer wished to be a free man in his profession, he must first amass five million dollars; his fortune would be his independence. This he himself proceeded methodically to do, succeeding in his early middle years. He deliberately sought wealth for the power that came with possession. He used his money, too, to provide his family generously with the comforts of life. For instance, almost the first thing he did was buy houses for his mother and his two sisters.

"He bought his mother a house many years before he bought one for himself." His daughter chuckled as in retrospect she could see the funny side of their life under the matriarch's rule. "We lived there with my grandmother for some time. She was a wonderful old character, but oh how dictatorial! We children suffered her discipline. In spite of her love of authority, a quality in which her son resembled her so closely, those two got along beautifully. When finally we did move into our own home, he drove up every single morning the distance of several miles to spend some time with her. He loved her dearly. I always thought it was remarkable that such dominating personalities got along so well."

In the same patriarchal spirit, he bought each of his two sisters a house on Ninety-second Street, in New York, with a large part of the fabulous fee he earned by one brilliant performance, at the age of twenty-eight. He had crossed the ocean with options from several United States breweries in which he wanted a British banking firm to invest. Unable to get an interview, he burst in upon a bank directors' meeting and announced, "Gentlemen, five minutes of your time!" After they had recovered from their surprise, they yielded to his demand for conference and, at the end of twenty-four hours, he had put over the kind of deal that helped him amass his first million dollars before he was thirty.

However, this deal was by no means Untermyer's first money-making triumph. He grew wealthy during his first year of law practice, at twenty-one. When he was twenty-four, he became famous the country over for a case he tried successfully, spending a hundred and six days at court. The decision set a precedent in making an attorney personally responsible for damages as the result of advising clients to commit a fraud. The eyes of great financiers and bankers now turned in Untermyer's direction. Youth that he was, he found himself catapulted into prominence and swamped with cases—perplexing, complicated problems that industrial leaders of the day had hesitated to entrust to the experienced legal moguls

of the times. Before he was twenty-five, he had a repu-
tation for having tried more cases in one year than any
other lawyer in New York.

Untermyer had hit his stride. Sought after by big
business interests, he offered his services at a huge price.
His skill was for sale to those who could afford it. He was
coming to the second great change in his life. In his
adolescence, he had changed from a mild, happy-go-lucky
lad to a serious student. Now in his early thirties, he
became intensely ambitious. He developed an obsession
for work—gruelling, feverish work that kept him at high
tension for sixteen, eighteen, or more hours each day
throughout his middle years. Large corporations, promi-
nent personalities, earnest judges, all claimed a share of
the great lawyer's time, for he had reached the pinnacle
of his performance as an attorney, surpassing any of his
contemporaries. He lengthened his days by rising at four
o'clock, dictating from his room by five o'clock and working on legal documents several hours before arriving at
his office in the early morning. Untermyer attributed his
early rising to asthma and insomnia, but as he lived to be
eighty-one, these ailments could not have been very serious. He resented time wasted in sleep. Four or five hours
were all that he gave up of each day for such refreshment.

His independence assured, Untermyer now began to
disclose new facets in his nature. From being altogether
the cold, cut-and-dried attorney, with services for sale to
anyone with a legitimate private claim, he awoke to a
realization that he could use his abilities for crusading
purposes. He labored harder and longer for the State of
New York, without any fee, than any other attorney had
ever done. The record of his battles against injustices
by big business interests is the most prolific record of his

life. Before we go into this stage of Samuel Untermyer's career, let us go back to his origins and get a perspective of this uncommon personality.

Isador Untermyer, Samuel's father, was a tobacco planter in Lynchburg, Virginia, who owned twelve hundred slaves at the time of his son's birth, in 1858. He felt a deep loyalty to the South, where, as a Jewish immigrant from Bavaria, he had been able to establish himself comfortably within a short time. When the Civil War broke out, he was made a lieutenant in the Confederate army, and invested all his money in the Confederacy—all, that is, except ten thousand dollars in gold that his cool-headed wife had silently stowed away in a New York bank against the unmentionable eventuality of a Confederate defeat. There was a large family to feed, and Mrs. Untermyer loved her children too dearly to submerge her maternalism altogether in loyalty to the cause of the South. Samuel, however, aped his father in this respect. He remembers one day, when he was seven, that as the Union army marched into Lynchburg, he ran up and down in front of his home shouting brazenly, "Hurrah for Jeff Davis!" then President of the Confederacy. The world was to thrill to this triumphant championing of unpopular causes for many a day in Samuel's later life.

Isador Untermyer, whose heart was weak, dropped dead at the news of Lee's surrender. His wife promptly gathered her brood of six children—four boys and two girls—and moved to New York. Going straight to a wealthy residential section of the city, she opened a boarding house, which immediately became the refuge of the many new arrivals in New York who had fled the defeated South and who had known the Untermyers back home. Having invested her savings in this enterprise, Mrs. Untermyer was left without any reserve to care for her six children, and the family experienced several years of comparative insecurity after the comfort to which they had been accustomed in the South. She was determined, however, that all four sons should get a college education. Samuel attended the free public schools of the city until he was twenty, when the family's improved finances and his own part-time job made it possible for him to enter Columbia Law School.

At twenty-two, he married Minnie Carl, a Protestant. The difference in their religion caused no disharmony between them, for he was devoted to her and to his three children. Commenting on the success of this interfaith marriage, his daughter, Mrs. Stanley Richter, described her father's religious philosophy:

"He was tolerant of all religions, but believed that one should give enough attention to the precepts and teachings of some particular church so that his conduct might be guided by it. It didn't matter so much which church. In our family he rather left it to my mother to see that we got a technical religious training. I do remember that after his own mother died he went to the Jewish Temple regularly once a week. He was devoted to her, and he seemed to be able to release this great filial loyalty in the spiritual atmosphere of the Temple.

"Did he ever mention any youthful ambition he had harbored, other than to be a lawyer?"

"Why, yes, he used to think as a boy that he would some day study to become a great Rabbi. Actually," Mrs. Richter smiled indulgently. "it was his love of declamation, his interest in dramatics, and a little hint of the reforming spirit, I think, that sought expression through the medium of rabbinical authority. I don't believe he ever considered that ambition very seriously. He did love to act, though. All through my girlhood, I remember how he would suddenly burst forth with the words of Bullwer or some such romantic poet.

"He liked the theater, particularly Booth. He went to all the Shakespearean plays he had time for, and said later that the modern theater was a degeneration of the art. In his reading, too, he chose the most romantic tales. You see, he was at heart a great sentimentalist, forced by his work to squelch his sentimentalism. But it sought expression in his choice of the theater for recreation and in his relationship with his family."

We discussed one of Untermyer's few hobbies, that of raising orchids in his suburban estate in Yonkers. The press made much of this orchid fancying of the master legal mind. He always came to court wearing one of his little orchids, and frequently, at noon, his chauffeur would come into the courtroom carrying a damp bag containing a fresh orchid. This indulgence provided a form of relaxation from a morning's ordeal of examining shrewd business magnates on the witness stand. Untermyer did not appear to resent the bantering references of newspaper reporters to his devotion to orchids. In this respect, as in the expert timing of his court examinations, he seemed almost to be working for them. It is said that he would save up a special cluster of questions, then hurl them quickly at his witness so that a crucial admission would be made at the moment that the reporters had to rush to press with their stories. Thus, at noon they got their punch line for the evening paper, and toward evening Untermyer would again extract from his witness the punch line for the next morning's newspaper.

Another of Untermyer's rare pastimes was that of raising

prize collies.   J. P. Morgan's collies were world-renowned,
but Untermyer determined to present a superior collie.
These two tycoons had been fencing with each other for
years in the courts; now they substituted prize collies for
the swords of their verbal fencing bouts. Morgan was defeated at the kennel shows, just as he was defeated in court,
by the man whose ability he sullenly acknowledged, making no secret of his admiration. He closed his kennels, and
Untermyer then closed his. Untermyer's daughter related
that her mother had disliked keeping kennels and was glad
when the contests were over, for war had broken out, and
it seemed to her that money was better spent on feeding
the starving children of Europe than on raising prize dogs.
Many another wealthy family followed the example of
the Morgans and the Untermyers, with the result that
the price of collies dropped.   Two powerful men, indulg-
ing their mutual craving for competition, had suddenly
created a national fad and with equal dispatch had
buried it.

The story of his court battle against the House of Morgan is the story of the longest battle of Untermyer's career
—a battle against monopolistic abuses, waged gratis by
Untermyer as a servant of the people of the United States,
that resulted in the enactment of the liberal reform legislation of Wilson's administration.

It all started in 1911, when Untermyer made a public
address entitled, "Is There a Money Trust?"   Quite on
his own, he had been doing considerable research into the
causes of economic breakdown from which the country
was suffering.   In his address, he tried to show how much
of the country's wealth was concentrated in the hands of
a few industrialists in New York.   All other business in-

terests were operating in fear and trembling under the critical eye of this financially powerful group. It was they who decided to whom loans and credits were to be issued. They could push money around or they could pile it up within a single city, according to their selfish inclinations. This, Untermyer claimed, had contributed to the business panic of 1907 and the depression that followed. His sensational attack caused the House of Representatives to establish the Pujo Committee, named for its chairman, to investigate the financial practices of firms charged by Untermyer to be harboring a "money trust." Untermyer was made chief counsel. For months, he applied his skill to the investigation, examining such important witnesses as J. P. Morgan, John D. Rockefeller, Senior, George F. Baker, and other financial wizards and business potentates. At last, Untermyer produced the full report of facts and figures to substantiate the charges he had made in his famous speech on money trusts, to wit: eighteen financial institutions in the three cities of New York, Chicago, and Boston virtually constituted a money trust through interlocking directorates in a hundred and twenty-four corporations, with an aggregate capital of twenty-five billion dollars.

While he was waging this battle, the opposition plotted how they might discredit these findings by discrediting Untermyer's record as an attorney. They hired a battery of detectives to search every one of his previous legal actions for flaws in the conduct of his profession. These investigations produced a biographical record of Samuel Untermyer that actually comprised forty volumes, now gathering dust in a safe deposit vault. This mass of data revealed only one item, in which Untermyer was but indirectly involved, that was open to some question. His enemies tried to persuade the Pujo Committee and the public that this vaguely recorded incident cast a shadow across the lawyer's impeccable record. But Untermyer's explanation conclusively wiped out any implication of guilt. Delighted with the marvelous record that Untermyer's enemies had thus unwittingly unfolded before the nation, the Committee gave him a vote of confidence and ordered him to proceed.

The fact that his behavior was irreproachable was, some say, the real secret of Untermyer's strength. Because he never needed to fear attack by his enemies, he was free to attack and pursue them relentlessly. That he was aware of the strength of utter veracity is revealed further in a remark he once made about a witness he was cross-examining, namely that he was handicapped because "the man is honest." His method was to dig for the first fragment of untruth, and then blast a charge wide open.

As a result of the Pujo Committee's investigations, the Federal Reserve Bank law was passed in 1913. Untermyer helped in the framing and passage of this law, which ensured the flow of money through the states wherever it was most needed. Other direct outcomes of the investigation were the Clayton Anti-Trust Act and the Federal Trade Commission Bill, which Untermyer also helped to frame and have passed. He was a close friend of President Wilson, whom he supported in these and other reform measures throughout his administration.

These were the years when many of the luxurious resources of the New World were still untapped. Untermyer was one of the first lawyers to recognize the need for combinations of capital to carry on the vast industrial enterprises of a growing country. As a young lawyer he himself had helped to form such combinations, thereby acquiring the wherewithal to enjoy that independence he later needed in order to fight the same big business interests when they took advantage of their power.

In 1903, Untermyer launched a battle against Wall Street Stock Exchange abuses, directed against minority stockholders, that continued for thirty years. His enemies are still bitter over the fact that, in attacking large corporations, the great lawyer appeared to have bitten the hand that had fed him. But a fair examination of his career and of his own writings and addresses yields a perfectly satisfactory explanation of this apparent betrayal. Combinations that resulted in the promotion of important projects that contributed to the country's wealth and power were to Untermyer a good outcome of twentieth-century business acumen. But when these combinations were carried too far, producing monopolies so powerful that they operated unjustly against the average citizen, Untermyer felt that some governmental regulation was called for, and for fully five decades he offered his services to the Federal Government, to New York State, and to New York City, without fee, to help correct the evils of monopoly.

Untermyer served New York State through a housing investigation for Governor Lehman that split open a building trade and contractors' ring. This was followed by his backing of remedial housing legislation that set a pattern for many other states. For long years he fought to unify the New York City subways and preserve the five-cent fare. One day, lying half dead from overwork in a huge bed that had been excavated from the ruins of Pompeii, he had reporters of the New York papers called to his bedside, and treated them to a two-hour harangue about the transit situation and other public controversies.

Untermyer annexed himself to numerous causes and individual complaints of people who came to him, without any money, needing counsel. According to one writer, "Although an avowed opponent of socialistic theories, Untermyer's political philosophy was so liberal that he did not hesitate to defend individual Socialists and radicals when he believed that their rights had been attacked unjustly, and he denounced the expulsion of five Socialists from the New York State Assembly."

As the ecomonic structure of the country changed, Untermyer was aware of the need to look to the grievances of labor. In an address, in 1935, he said, "If I correctly appraise the trend of the times, the days of great fortunes and the exploitation of labor are over. Labor is about to receive a more just share of the wealth which it creates, but the principles of capitalism will survive." As part of this trend, he advocated government ownership of public utilities.

The spread of his interests is still further illustrated by his defense of Margaret Sanger, who was suffering a series of legal onslaughts for her courageous fight to increase the chances for life and health in the families of the poor by means of birth control, and was in need of an able spokesman to counteract the vitriolic attacks of a large group of misunderstanding people.

When Henry Ford issued articles in his paper, the *Dearborn Independent,* against the Jews, Untermyer, defending Herman Bernstein in his suit against the motor magnate, waged a relentless battle in the interests of religious tolerance. As a result, Ford made a public announcement that he had been misled by informants who had been untrustworthy, and agreed to destroy all traces of the libelous publications.

In 1934, early in the history of Hitler's assaults on freedom the world over, Untermyer was active as the first
president of the World Non-sectarian Anti-Nazi Council,
in their organized protest against Nazi persecutions.

People often wondered why Untermyer did not seek
public office. Twice he was offered the Tammany nomina-
tion for United States Senator, but declined, probably
preferring a career unsullied by the opportunism characteristic of politics. A reporter once asked him, as he was
strolling through his garden and showing off his orchids,
"Mr. Untermyer, is there any public office that you would
consider if it were offered to you?" His eyes twinkled as
he looked up from his flowers, and he made a facetious
confession, "Why yes. There is just one. I'd like to be
New York City's Park Commissioner."

Asked for the secret of his own success, Untermyer never
conceded that it was due to anything but hard work. His
co-workers found him absolutely indefatigable, almost in-
human in his persistence. He made many enemies, as
what great man does not, but he feared none. When he
met a capable adversary, he was gracious in his respect.
John D. Rockefeller, Senior, he declared to be such a one.
After badgering him for hours on the witness stand, he
would shake Rockefeller's hand in admiration.

Untermyer died at the age of eighty-one, after only a
brief retirement from a furiously active career. He had
tried to retire earlier a number of times, but was pushed
into action again and again because of his indignation at
the injustices that flourished for lack of a champion of
human welfare. He is remembered for his extensive service as such a champion, as much as for his profound ability
as a lawyer.

They Fight Leprosy

THE BUKER TWINS

ANY FOREIGN MISSIONARY is apt to seem a bit awesome to those of us who hug our own hearths. The missionary that I was to interview had just returned from some place that I could not even find on the map. I pictured a tall, ascetic creature who would speak patiently but with aloof dignity. Imagine my surprise when I was met by a friendly young American, about five feet seven, with a warm, humorous expression on his Yankee countenance! In a minute I felt that I had known this man for years, had chatted with him on the campus during school days. He had that kind of informality. His genial manner reflected a sense of complete oneness with his chosen work.

Dr. Richard Buker returned to the United States on furlough, while his brother remained to hold the fort in Kengtung State, below the Burma Road. War flared up there after he left, and at the time I met him he was unable to secure permission from government authorities to return with his wife and child. "Missionary folk are indifferent to personal danger," commented an official in the Mission Society, "but Dr. Buker and his wife haven't been able to convince the Government of that."

The territory in which the Buker brothers are established is only two hundred miles from Thailand, with whose geographical location the world has become grimly familiar. But before the present war, hardly anyone except a foreign missionary knew or cared about a place called "Kengtung State." There the brothers founded a leper colony, because the lepers came from miles around pleading for medical rather than religious ministry.

Richard Buker, the doctor, had to organize a medical school to teach the natives to become nurses and hospital assistants. In order to have the building put up in which the students were to be taught, he had to study the building trade. He learned the Lahu, Wa, and Shan languages, and translated medical books into these languages. In the matter of treatment, he had to fight the resistance of the natives, particularly with regard to modern concepts of nutrition. (Their idea of a good breakfast was beans and pickles, rather than milk and fruit juice.) His brother, Raymond, who studied for the ministry, likewise accepted the difficult call to Kengtung. His job is equally diversified, for he keeps books, teaches reading, stocks the larder, irons out human relationships, and supervises a staff of native assistants. Both doctor and minister, in their capacities as foreign missionaries, may be found doing any job required to keep a community going. At all times they are sustained by the conviction that they were chosen by the Lord to bring to these people, many of whom were abandoned because of their dread disease, the surcease of Christian ministry.

Richard and Raymond are twins, the sixth and seventh children in a family of eight. All their lives they worked and played together. "We quarreled between us when we were very little, but the minute some outsider tried to champion one against the other, both of us turned on him with fury and told him to stay out of our business," the doctor recalled. He speaks of this fraternal relationship as though it were all a part of the Lord's design, for it required close and faithful teamwork to make any strides among the unyielding Shan people.

When first the world heard of the Buker twins, it was in the field of athletics, a field far removed from the treatment of leprosy in a semi-civilized community. At nineteen Raymond was well known in New England as a runner, having won the Maine Intercollegiate Cross-Country championship. Two years later, he won the International two-mile race in nine minutes, twenty-five and three fifths seconds. In the Olympics of 1924, he was the only American to place in the fifteen-hundred-meter event.

"Were you a runner too?" I prodded, as the doctor seemed to dwell on his brother's achievements rather than on his own.

"In 1920, when we were both in Bates College in Maine, we tied for the Intercollegiate championship. We had arranged that tie between us. We just decided that we would run up ahead until we got where nobody was pushing us, and then we would tie."

The twins have been "tying" ever since, except that in their missionary work there is no holding back, for the exigencies of the disease they are out to combat forces them to push on to more and more distant goals.

"How did you happen to develop such skill as runners? Were you interested in athletics in general at school?"

"We were, but we never could get into anything because we were both small and thin. In fact, we were about the smallest boys in school. We liked basketball, football, and baseball, but nobody wanted us to join in those activities, with the result that we were developing quite a sense of inferiority until it occurred to us that in running there would always be room for us in the rear even if there was no place up front, and so we went out for this sport. We just kept at it, with an enormous stick-to-it-iveness that we had inherited from our mother and our beloved aunt. Before long we discovered we were good at running. Running is easier for those who start to practice while very young."

"But you boys were in high school before you started, weren't you?"

"Officially, as athletic contestants, yes. But we started running when we were six. It was a mile to school and a mile back, and we usually ran all the way—he hesitated—back. When we were about ten, we started to deliver newspapers. That meant getting up early and going over our routes before school opened, and took a lot of running up- and downhill. Although the family later owned a bicycle, it had to be shared among five brothers, and that left us on our feet most of the time.

"Now there are two other things that are necessary besides perseverance and early training: good meals and regular sleep and rest. My mother saw to those. She was a staunch disciplinarian, who insisted on our nine o'clock bedtime even when we were in high school. She had a good understanding of nutrition and fed us wisely. All in all, we were pretty thoroughly trained in preparation for that Olympic record."

The twins regarded their athletic achievements as activities of boyhood. It served to rid them of their sense of inferiority. But after a brief period as famed milers, they were ready to give up running for a career of service.

Raymond had known ever since he was ten that he

would be a minister. Richard had the same ambition, but it was feared that his speaking voice was not strong enough. In looking for another opportunity to be of service, he then thought of emulating their family physician, Dr. Arnold, who used to travel for miles over bad roads in winter to attend a sick child in the Buker home. The doctor always refused a fee, for the father of the twins was a minister who supported his large family as well as he could on four hundred dollars a year.

There was a period, after the boys were graduated from the Mount Hermon Prep School, when they did not believe they would go to college. They attended business school for a month and then, at eighteen, decided to join the Army. But Raymond was refused because of a slight rupture, and the interviewing army officer tore up Richard's application, saying, "You don't want to go without your brother, do you?" Richard realized suddenly that that was true. What now? What money they had saved from previous earnings had given out. First of all, they decided, they needed to earn some money. They knocked around at all sorts of odd jobs, working as stokers in a Navy yard, as laborers in a shipyard, as riveters on submarines, as cooks at conferences, and as farm hands on the wheat fields of North Dakota. These jobs were a little more lucrative than some of the work they had done at sixteen, such as digging ditches and fitting pipes for a water company, but still they were getting nowhere. The period of intellectual incubation came to an end, and both boys made up their minds to go back to school. They went to Bates College, in Maine.

"How did you manage with the tuition?" I asked.

Richard leaned back in his chair, folded his hands and

half-shut his eyes. He spoke in a soft, reminiscent tone:

"Now take this down about my Aunt Eva, because I just feel like telling the whole true story. Aunt Eva Buker was an old maid, a schoolteacher in Lewiston, Maine. She left there and came to New York to study in a normal school, and went to Germany for a full year to continue her studies. When she returned, she was assigned the position of Vice-principal of Brooklyn Training School in New York. She retired in 1918.

Aunt Eva had always admired her brother, my father, for his sacrificial willingness to serve in the ministry in rural communities. Father was a Baptist minister, pastor of three country churches, and superintendent of thirteen schools in Foster, Rhode Island. He believed in serving these rural communities, even at a great loss of income. His earnings never rose above six hundred dollars a year, which went to support a family of five boys and three girls. Aunt Eva felt it was her responsibility to help him educate his children. It was her money that enabled us to go to Mount Hermon Prep School, a truly remarkable institution, and when we were ready for college, she decided to enter her retirement from teaching in order to make a home for my brother and myself in Maine, where we enrolled in Bates College. I just can't say too much for my Aunt Eva, a woman of great wisdom and a very level head, who started with absolutely nothing and succeeded at a fine career."

As the details of a life story are thus laid out, you can see how many seemingly unrelated events have a converging influence and suddenly develop the nucleus of a man's career. I believe that Richard Buker told me the story of his aunt because he felt that the Lord had used her in

guiding him toward his work in the leprosy-ridden fast-
nesses below the Burma Road. The youths had been
using up time in what appeared to be purposeless en-
deavors. But in the background stood Aunt Eva, ready
to start them off on their last mile of preparation toward
their lifework.

The years spent at Bates College are a happy memory
to both men. Raymond was President of the Y.M.C.A.
there, member of the Student Council, pastor of a church,
and captain of the track team. Scholastically, he was always ahead of his brother, which didn't bother Richard in
the least; in fact he is proud of his brother's superiority. I
was treated to a full story of Richard's own ability, courage, and religious zeal later when I visited the offices of the
Mission to Lepers and of the American Baptist Mission.

In 1924, Raymond wrote to Joseph Robbins, foreign
secretary and chairman of a Student Volunteer Conven-
tion where the two men had met, as follows: "It may help
you to remember me if I remind you that I am the champion two-miler of America. On the 4th of July I am to
run one more race in San Francisco. Then I wish to go
to the most difficult foreign mission field in the world."
He was speaking for Richard as well, for he expected his
brother to join him on this venture.

The Bukers were sent to Kengtung State in Burma to do
general missionary work there. This is an area about the
size of Massachusetts. The people here are divided into
two distinctly different types. The Shan, or the valley
people, belong to a civilization more ancient than China's.
They have resisted stubbornly the efforts of the missionaries to change their habits. The hill people, both the
Lahu's and the Wa's, have responded eagerly to the Chris-

tian philosophy of service and equality among one's fellow men. The Buddhist philosophy is to ignore the sufferer and deal with the survivor. In a land where disease is rampant, this philosophy of the survival of the fittest has meant great hardship and torment, especially for those afflicted with the world's most feared disease, leprosy. Victims are often ostracized, driven out of their homes, and forsaken even by their families.

When the stricken natives in that semi-civilized state heard about the doctor who had arrived from the American Mission, they dragged themselves on foot over great distances to see him. But Dr. Buker was not equipped to care for and treat these diseased and homeless wanderers, for he had been assigned a general medical program for the state and was unprepared to devote himself exclusively to leprosy. He did not see, at the time, how he would be able to turn his attention to this particular disease, knowing well the extent of the undertaking. He tried to make some explanation to the natives who came to him, advising them to return, but he dared not even ask himself where they should go. At last his spirit rebelled against dealing out such a cruel mandate. It happened when a leper came to him, after having traveled eight days on foot, bringing with him his three children. The rains were about due, and Dr. Buker shrank from sending the family back. Suddenly he felt impelled to accept this challenge that he had been warding off for three years. He now believes that when he decided then and there to treat this man, his first leper patient, he did so by divine guidance. He knew intuitively that he was assuming a responsibility that would grow quickly into a vast project in the Shan State of Kengtung, Burma.

The treatment of leprosy is a long, arduous process. At the time the Bukers first began it, less than one tenth of the patients could be cured—"arrested" is the word they prefer to use. As lepers often live out their normal life span, they require treatment for years and years. There were parts of that territory where the disease attacked as many as sixteen per cent of the population; nowhere was its incidence less than three per cent. Where would the man power and the money come from to cope with such a problem? But even before these difficulties were seriously thought of, the first leper colony had virtually been established. It was a colony situated in the graveyard— "Well, you know, the people there never object." News traveled fast that the American doctor was treating lepers. They came from all over the area. In describing his first colony, Dr. Buker said, "I could stand on the city wall and I could speak to my wife in our backyard, and I could speak over her to the lepers in the leper colony. Every single day of our lives lepers came up over the city wall and sat in our backyard."

"There is one question I want to ask you especially, and all my readers will want to know," I ventured apologetically. In the face of his courage and self-denial, I was a little ashamed of my question. "Weren't you afraid you would contract the disease? And your wife—what of the danger to her?"

His eyes glinted knowingly. Always he is asked that question. He had his reply ready. Becoming slightly official for the first time, he explained, "The doctor is not afraid of any sickness that does not kill a person within two or three days. The only diseases that are frightening are plague and typhus. He is no more afraid of leprosy than you are of contracting tuberculosis by being near or touching a tuberculous person. Both diseases are very similar. Books wrongly give the impression that leprosy is highly contagious. It is anything but that. Only ten per cent of leprosy cases are infectious. Leprosy is very hard to contract, almost impossible. It progresses very slowly and is rarely fatal. Patients die of other causes while they are ill with leprosy. It attacks the skin and the nerves. There are people who are susceptible to it and who will contract it under certain circumstances, just as there are people who will succumb to the tuberculosis germs in their environment. Most people living in the same environment remain well because their bodies can resist the bacilli."

"You speak of treatment—what has been done? Has a cure been found for the disease?"

"From fifty to eighty-five per cent of the cases can be arrested—not cured—depending on how early a diagnosis is made. The first sign of the disease is a sense of numbness on some part of the body. If we can get a person at this stage, he can be successfully treated. Those who are in the work can be examined rigidly every six months for the possible discovery of such numb spots. Treatment consists of injecting an antitoxin. For some time Chaulmoogra oil was used. I have been using oil of Hydnocarpus. The study of leprosy has advanced more rapidly in the past twenty years than ever before. Men like Dr. Oberdoerffer and Dr. Collier have been devoting most of their lives to it. As far as is now known, there is no absolute cure for leprosy. Some patients get well by themselves, without treatment."

"Why does it occur only in certain parts of the world?"

"We are not sure, but two causes are suspected. It may be a nutritional disease, or it may be due to contagion. Both causes are being thoroughly investigated by medical science." Dr. Buker is himself working hard on the problem.

The years spent at odd-job labor in the United States proved of great value to the twins, for they were often called upon to apply the knowledge and skills they had acquired in building houses and running kitchens in Keng-tung. Even Richard's experience in milking cows one summer, at the age of thirteen, was to serve him in good stead here. "The natives don't ordinarily drink milk, you know," he explained. "But we found that good nutrition was one of the important elements in fighting leprosy. I had to buy a herd of buffaloes and teach the natives how to milk them. I myself always liked milking; in fact, still help out when necessary."

It soon became apparent that more facilities were needed than could be provided in their first graveyard colony. The American Mission to Lepers sent a sizable gift to the Bukers, enabling them to build two model brick houses. Their plan was to house four lepers in each, and as more money was appropriated, they planned to build more such houses.

Dr. Buker came to America to speak on his work among the diseased, hoping thereby to raise additional funds for the colony. How the money was secured is another of the many coincidences in a life given to service. A strange man telegraphed Dr. Buker, asking for an appointment. The stranger took down the facts about the leper work, saying that he represented some woman who was prepared to contribute to the project. This woman, who had read of the Kengtung Mission, donated four thousand dollars. The doctor returned to his colony full of new enthusiasm.

Within seven years the colony comprised thirty-five brick buildings. As the sick people began to crowd into the one place where they could get help, it became apparent that outlying colonies would have to be established to prevent congestion in so small an area. In one section of the land, whole villages were infected, and it was there that the next colony was established. The first white man to help in this work was an American missionary who had himself been afflicted with the disease and was therefore willing to work among the patients. Some twenty-six natives, the more intelligent of the patients, were selected and given a medical course in order that they might help in their own colonies.

All the patients work to help support their colony. Some grow vegetables, others fish, and still others help in the construction work. With a job to do and the knowledge that they are members of a community, these people can live out their lives in comparative peace and happiness, even if they are never able to leave the colony. "The secret of our success," Dr. Buker tells American co-workers, "has been the happiness we have been able to bring to the patients. Throw away medicine, half the rice, all the money that is given them in lieu of treatment in some places, but give them happiness by restoring their sense of importance, and their condition will respond to treatment."

Perhaps the best picture of the life among these people can be seen from this story that Dr. Buker related about the Lahu boy, David:

"David was given a better education than most Lahu

boys because he seemed a promising lad. In lower Burma, he worked in the family of the missionary who had charge of the mission school and learned the peculiar habits of the white man. He learned how particular the white man is about his water, how clean one must be to handle food properly. He acquired the extreme politeness of the Indian toward the white man.

"The First World War broke out, and David became a soldier. Here he learned discipline such as a Lahu never dreams of in his native haunts. At the cessation of the war, David went back to school and studied to be a preacher. He learned to read and write English. He returned to his home the best-trained preacher in all Lahu land. More than this, David had developed character. He had learned to think for himself, for his people; even when the white missionary suggested unwise procedures, David had the courage to object if he thought they were unwise. This characteristic is very rare among the native people of Burma.

"David married. Three children blessed his home. One day he went hunting, and he scratched his forehead. The scratch above his eye and beside his ear failed to heal quickly, so he came to the hospital for treatment. After a careful examination, I was gravely suspicious. The area was numb, as well as red and raised. Examination of the skin under the microscope revealed one germ that looked like the leper germ. David was a leper.

"I called David to his house. Together we prayed; then I revealed the fact to him. Oh the anguish in his voice as he cried, 'It cannot be. It cannot be! Of all the diseases in the world, I have vowed that if I became a leper, I would go to the jungles and take my own life.' For a long time I talked with David. I explained that if only he would accept his condition, God would give him grace to stand it. There was a great need in the nine leper colonies for a Christian leader. More than this, modern treatment held out hope for a cure in such an early case as his. For two weeks, David went into the jungles to fight with himself. Finally he came back victorious, resigned to the will of God. Humbled, he said he would go and work with those he had feared most in all his life, those he had done everything possible to avoid. It had been the greatest testing time of his whole life.

"Months passed; the best treatment was given him, and he responded. There were one or two periods when the disease seemed to get much worse. But after eighteen months, his case was arrested. Sundays and weekdays he now leads the people in the leper colonies in the everlasting truths found in Christ. Who is better fitted to do this than one who has gone through the deep waters of adversity?"

Raymond Buker, the minister, conducts Bible schools with the patients in the colonies. He speaks four or five different dialects in two languages. He teaches bright lepers to read in one week by a new method of teaching the main sounds. He also teaches them to write. Christianity is revealed to them in the attitude of the American missionaries who are treating them; it is not an alien religion that they are told they must accept. Gradually, however, they do accept it, won over by example rather than by preaching.

Richard has spent his furlough in the United States attending Harvard Medical School, where he has since received his doctorate in public health. While in this country he has given frequent talks on his work with the lepers, and some who have heard him have been moved to give their support. His wife and their three children are here with him, but the entire family will return again to the stricken land they have adopted for their own.

Both men lay no claim to greatness. They consider themselves ordinary people with perhaps more than average determination to make the most of their abilities. Through perseverance and self-discipline the Buker twins became famous as runners, and these very traits have enabled them to make great strides in improving the lot of a neglected people.

I looked at the doctor's calm, smiling face. A life of service has kept it boyish and young. Again I had the feeling that we were school chums, relaxing after some games on the college campus. He looked as though his life were as easy and delightful as all that.

"Remember the Name"

LESLIE MACMITCHELL

WAR BETWEEN JAPAN AND OUR COUNTRY had just begun the day I set out to interview Leslie Mac-
Mitchell. An airplane was put-putting like a motorboat,
flying low over his home on Eighty-seventh Street, New
York. People in the streets were talking of air-raid alarms
and, as I mounted the stone steps and rang the bell, I
wondered whether MacMitchell, then almost twenty-one,
would not be too excited over his impending role in the
Army to care to talk to me about track. The basement
door opened and my host, looking up at me standing on
the steps, said with quiet dignity, "We live down here."

I was escorted through the dark hallway into a living-
dining room. How shall I describe to you the peace and
warmth of that atmosphere which gave me such a cozy,
tucked-in, Christmas Day sensation? In the center of the
room was a large, old-fashioned dining-room table. Leslie's
books and typewriter were on it, and it was obvious that
I had interrupted him at his homework. He introduced
his mother, who gave me one friendly, eager look and then
sat down in an old rocker and readjusted the radio so
that it should not disturb us. It was turned to a symphony
number. Leslie explained, "I don't mind if the radio
plays while I study. If it's classical music, it doesn't disturb me."

The room glinted and sparkled in spite of its plain

furniture and old textiles. At once I realized that the glow came from the trophies Leslie had won all over the country. Dozens of them were artistically arranged on a low chest against one wall, while a small table supported an overflow of several more, all beautiful in line and texture. It was fitting that these trophies should be arrayed thus alone, in a room furnished from necessity in a simple, unobtrusive key.

We talked for a while about some of those trophies. Leslie appreciates their artistic worth, admiring them objectively. As he lifted each one, he mentioned the place from which it came. Not once, in an evening's conversation, did he use the words, "I won." He is the most modest of individuals about his running. His mother, too, as she sat in the rocker and watched her son, refrained from making a single laudatory comment about his achievements as the greatest national cross-country runner of our day, the man who finished second to Cunningham in the Metropolitan A.A.U. when he was but seventeen, with only a year's training.

"What makes a good runner," I asked, remembering the words of another champion miler to the effect that anyone can be trained to run.

"Well, health and training are important, but you've got to have natural ability," MacMitchell replied. "Now there are some fellows down at the school who work just as hard at it as I do, but they don't have as much natural ability. By that I mean endurance and speed. Still, some of those boys may have more ambition than I have."

It is true that Leslie doesn't give the impression of having submerged himself in the business of maintaining cross-country records to the exclusion of every other occupation. He retained a scholastic average of around ninety at New York University, where he was a Senior at the time of our interview, in spite of the fact that more than two hours of his time each day have been taken up with training. He travels more than an hour extra in the city's subway to get his training every day. In addition to daily calisthenics, he does six to eight miles of running to keep in trim. At college he majored in physical education, which he hopes to teach. Of his other school subjects he likes sociology best, "largely because we had such a good instructor in that."

During his college course, Leslie earned a little by working during the registration periods and as usher at the basketball and football games. A Charles Hayden scholarship provided his tuition, which would otherwise have been prohibitive. Summers he worked at a boys' camp. He knew that he would have to earn money immediately upon graduation, but apparently he was not looking for a "cushy" job that might be handed to him for the sake of his fame as a runner. He was thoughtful but not discouraged as he stated his plan for teaching physical education, having just learned that New York would not be giving any civil service examinations for physical education teachers for a while.

"But surely you should have no trouble getting a job as coach," I suggested, surprised that he seemed unaware of the gilded prospects open to him as soon as he was graduated.

"I don't particularly care for a job just to coach and nothing else," he answered. "I'd really like to teach physical education. But of course, now with the war on, I don't know what will happen anyway."

His mother, who works as housekeeper for a doctor, appears equally uninterested in having her son cash in on his sport laurels. They both plan in terms of honest work at honest pay. She was much more concerned over the fact that, although Leslie had only half a year of college to go before getting his degree, the war might prevent his completing the course.

MacMitchell, by technical standards, is only a cub as a miler. Given training up to the time he is twenty-five—the best age for runners—and coaches say that he is sure to be the first man to make a mile in four minutes straight. They say this because he ran up a record in George Washington High School at seventeen for 4:19, which is considerably better than Cunningham, whose best schoolboy effort was 4:27.7.

During our interview, a middle-aged man entered the apartment as freely as a member of the family, and Mrs. MacMitchell greeted him with, "Hello, Tom." Leslie introduced me to Mr. Greenwald. I realized that this was Coach Greenwald of Leslie's high-school days, who, against his own modest aspirations, had induced him to try for the cross-country run. He had spotted the boy as a runner when he was but fifteen. A year later, when Leslie came back from camp weighing 175 pounds, he told him he would have to run off twenty pounds, as that was too much weight for his height of five feet, eleven inches. While practicing his reducing exercises, Leslie was surprised to find how easily he could run three, four, and even five miles, and he realized that Coach Greenwald might be right. That started him off as a cross-country runner, known today as "Kid Mercury" and "Wonder Horse."

Leslie was born in New York, and was only nine when

his father, a Scottish mechanic, died. He and his mother have been close companions ever since, struggling through a long depression to get the best that New York has to offer a young, studious, and serious-minded boy in the way of a college education. Leslie's boyhood sports included practically everything except running. His early training was on the city streets or in Van Cortlandt Park. He enjoyed hockey, baseball, swimming, and practically every other sport, but he never thought of track until the opportunity to run was presented one summer when he went to camp. As a matter of fact, a condition in his heels, left from the time he had diphtheria as a child of seven, makes it painful for him to wear the ordinary light running shoe. He has to cut out the backs of these shoes when he runs. He lands first on the ball of his foot, then lightly on the heel, and just as the heel touches ground he springs onto the other foot. He makes an initial dash for first place in order that he can stay on the inside of the track, where he has the shortest run, and is not disturbed by other flying elbows. There he remains to the end of the race, usually.

In his last college cross-country race in November, 1941, Leslie MacMitchell was the first runner ever to take the Freshman and three Varsity crowns. Only John Paul Jones of Cornell won three times, in 1910, 1911, and 1912. They had no Freshman race in those years, so that Leslie's record stands unequaled.

He won the Wanamaker mile race in February, 1942, in what was described as "the good but far from extraordinary time of 4:11.3." Before the race he had remarked blandly, "There are too many angles to be considered before thinking of records." Coach von Elling at New York University commented, "I won't try to advise him. He's proved very good at solving his own problems."

But neither triumphs nor publicity have gone to Mac-Mitchell's head. A sports writer in a Metropolitan newspaper wrote, "You might conclude that under such bombast Leslie is running up a full set of tin ears. Such is not the case. Records and their running supposedly leave him twitching about as furiously as a bag of cement. He says he runs to win, not to break records."

Although he dreams of a four-minute mile for himself, Leslie still misses a streetcar if he has to run for it with books in his hands. On the street he wears rubber-soled shoes against the hard pavement. Coach von Elling has mapped out a plan for the favorite in his patient, persevering way. "Give Mac another two years, and he'll make Cunningham's 4:04.4 look silly." Von Elling thinks what he needs to practice is pacing himself. Cunningham practically carried a stopwatch in his head.

Leslie thinks a lot of his coach. He likes his democratic method of training. "There are all kinds of coaches," he explained. "Some of them tell you to do this or not to do that. Von Elling believes in letting us work out for ourselves just what is best for us. Then, if we come up against a problem that calls for help, he is there to discuss it with us."

"Why does everybody want to know what I eat?" Leslie turned toward his mother, smiling, when I asked if he had to stick to a strict diet. "Naturally I don't try any new kinds of foods just before a race, not knowing whether or not they will agree with me. But that's about all."

His mother, however, supplemented this with some significant remarks. "You see, we're Scottish, and the

Scottish people never go in for rich gravies and heavy sauces. We just eat our food in its natural state, as it comes. Leslie never seemed to care for pie at all, and only once in a while does he eat a piece of cake. He's awfully found of fruit, eats lots of it. I usually have cooked fruit for dessert. He drinks about a quart of milk a day."

The Champ eats three hours before a race, and usually it is steak, potatoes, and a green vegetable. He never drinks anything but milk. As a child, he once tasted tea and coffee, and didn't like either one. As for alcohol, he says—with some feeling for him, for he usually speaks mildly—"Why, I can't even bear the smell of it."

"What do you do when you go out on a social engagement?" I asked, knowing that among the sophisticated New York college crowd there is a large group that cannot do without its highballs and cocktails. "Well, if the girl I'm with drinks, she orders a drink and then, when she sees that I don't take one, she usually doesn't want another. Sometimes, when there are just the two of us, she doesn't drink at all. But when we're in a group, as at a tea dance on Sunday, it seems natural for a girl to do what the rest of the crowd does, even if I don't join in."

The runner is a good-looking youth, on the Gary Cooper style—rugged, shy, serious, but with an easy grace and a twinkle in his eye that seems to say life is not too baffling an adventure. His face is lean, with an interesting bone structure that causes large, flat shadows on his cheeks. He has a steady, kindly gaze, and speaks with a quiet poise surprising in so young and unassuming a person. He is very sure of himself, but not the least bit vain.

MacMitchell is used to the hard way. He lost the Wana-maker mile race in 1940 because he was suffering from intestinal influenza at the time; but not wanting to make excuses to anybody, he had kept it a secret. Never coddled in his boyhood, he possesses amazing strength. Von Elling says, "I've never seen him finish a race exhausted. He has an amazing heartbeat of thirty-eight. Cunningham's was forty. The low pulse indicates superb physical condition, easing pressure on the heart during exertion."

Although his strength is largely responsible for the fact that MacMitchell has never lost one of the thirty-four cross-country races in which he has competed, it was apparent to me as I studied his and his mother's statements and observed the well-regulated home atmosphere that such physical well-being was by no means an accident. This young man has no habit that might impair his health. He retires at about ten-thirty or eleven. He never goes out the evening before a race. He doesn't smoke. "It's never been proved that smoking is definitely harmful. Lots of my friends smoke a little," he says with tolerance, "but I just never started. And I know there's a poison in tobacco, so I don't deliberately try to acquire the habit."

Leslie MacMitchell gets fan mail from all over the country. Girls ask for his photograph. The head of the Department of Publicity at New York University had small ones made up, so that they could easily be slipped into an ordinary envelope, for Leslie began to worry over the cost of mailing out larger ones in manila envelopes. Pennies count in the Champ's life, and he is neither ashamed nor embarrassed to admit it. Yet he continues to scorn any chance of capitalizing on his athletic prowess, seeking to earn his way in the world on his own merits as an honest, likable, normal boy.

Let My People Go

PAUL ROBESON

PEOPLE SAY no one is a great person in his own family. That adage was not true of Paul Robeson. His whole family adored him and treated him as a special gift of God. It started when Paul was first born, a late child. His mother was nearing fifty and quite ill. The family did not expect such a big, healthy, happy baby. Three older brothers and an older sister doted on him. His mother's last years were lightened by his laughter. She died when he was seven.

The story of Paul Robeson's childhood was given to me by his brother, the Reverend B. C. Robeson, pastor of a New York church. Later, his wife went over the narrative with me and gave me some additional items. Paul himself was away on a long concert tour, but I was lucky to get from his brother, who still dotes on him, the unique kind of story that another member of an artist's family can tell.

I had heard about the singer's self-deprecating modesty. His brother revealed as he talked a remarkable insight into the way Paul functions. Some of the little incidents he related might have seemed irrelevant if it had been Paul talking about himself for the great singer is forever under a compulsion to discharge his heaven-sent gift upon an avid world. He has no time to analyze the daily incidents of his life and to ruminate upon their significance.

To Paul himself, it sometimes appears that he fairly blundered his way to greatness. He had made several starts on a number of different paths in his youth. He had won acclaim as an athlete, an honor student, an orator, an actor, and a singer. He intended studying for the ministry, but then switched to law. But he always knew of his "luck," as he puts it. When Paul was still at Rutgers University, Alexander Woollcott met him and made this analysis: "I felt at the time that I had just crossed the path of someone touched by destiny. He was a young man on his way. He did not know where he was going, but never in my life have I seen anyone so quietly sure, by some inner knowledge, that he was going somewhere."

Paul's mother was part Indian and part Quaker. Although Paul was but seven when she died, he mentions two traits that he thinks he got from her: To his Indian heritage, he attributes the need to lock himself up in his room for days at a time, to escape from friends and society. To his Quaker heritage, he attributes his belief in divine guidance whenever he is faced with a decision to make. He may refuse an offer to perform for several thousands of dollars, and then appear at a concert without being paid because he is "following the gleam." Guided by this intuition, he has used his gift of song to help many causes. The Negroes say Paul Robeson's influence is greater than that of writers, anthropologists, and philosophers because of the way he interprets their songs. Knowing this, he sings wherever it will further his mission, whether or not he is paid for the performance.

Robeson has been a force to reckon with by all who are guilty of racial and religious prejudice. He says he is better able to appeal to white people because he spent a happy childhood among them. In the town of Somerville, New Jersey, where he went to high school, his father was a Presbyterian minister. This kindly old man had been a runaway slave at fifteen, and had put himself through Lincoln University, studying for the ministry. The world had given him a chance, and in his gratitude he had raised his family to be unconscious of any bitterness between the races. The family enjoyed respect and solicitude in the town.

Paul's friends were white and colored folk of the better-educated groups in the community. He was a popular visitor in any of their homes. Motherless, he had been raised in his childhood by "sisters" and kind neighbors, as well as a devoted family. He was truly a beloved child, and this gave his personality a radiant quality that won him friends of both races. When he grew up and received his first shock as a result of discrimination experienced in college, it was impossible for him to hate white people. Had he not known and made many friends among them? Although determined to combat discrimination, he always remained philosophical and tolerant about it. It will be different some day, he thinks, and in the meantime puts all his pleading for that difference into the song he sings to the thousands of white folk in his audience, "Let My People Go."

The Reverend Robeson told me that that trait of patient tolerance, waiting for the end of bondage, was passed on to them by their father. Paul's father seems to have been the original genius of the family, in the way he directed their home life after his wife died. "We all shared the work in the house, my father acting as manager, and that's how we kept our home together," Paul's brother

related. During the summer, the two older boys worked
in a brickyard or did odd jobs; and when Paul was nine
or ten, they let him help, watching that he didn't do too
much, for Paul was always such an energetic worker.
Money was never plentiful in the minister's family, so
it seemed natural that all the boys should be earning a
little for themselves. Their father made no issue of how
the money was to be used, but the boys generally gave him
their earnings and then received allowances. Every time
Paul's brother mentioned his father, it was only to show
how lightly the man had exercised that fatherly pre-
rogative of giving orders. The boys were free all day and
every day, but they were mature and dependable in
their use of it. They got no sermons about how to behave,
except the superbly effective one of seeing daily the perfect
example set for them by their father. The elder Robeson
did his share quietly. One of his humble chores was to
fill a big pot with whatever vegetables their own garden
yielded and place it on the stove to cook, just before he
left on his round of parish visits. That was to be dinner
for the evening.

"How is it," I asked Paul's brother, "that you haven't
mentioned any incident in Paul's youth in connection
with his voice?"

"We just didn't think it was important then. I can
remember, though, when we first had an inkling. W. D.
(the boys always refer to this eldest brother, who has since
died, by his initials), Paul, and I used to play baseball together. One day, when Paul was about ten, as we were
returning home from play, we were all singing together,
the same as usual. We were harmonizing that popular
song of the time, 'Down By the Old Mill Stream.' All of

a sudden W. D. stopped walking, turned around to Paul, and said, 'Say, boy, hit that chord again, will you?' Paul hit it again. 'Why Paul,' he exclaimed, with a leap of intuition, 'I believe you can sing!' Paul laughed. He figured we were just feeling good after a swell ball game.

"When we got home, W. D. made him sing 'Annie Laurie' by himself. That was the first time someone actually took time off just to listen to the boy's voice. When he finished, my brother said, 'As far as I'm concerned, you can have your musical diploma right now.' Then he went to my father and reported that Paul could sing. He got Paul to join the church choir, and encouraged him to sing solos. Father used to arrange church entertainments, and our whole family was corralled by him to help. After W. D. started to make a fuss over Paul's voice, Father had to let him sing all by himself occasionally at church concerts and on other occasions. Of course, we never thought of singing lessons."

One dark vision swept across the boy's bright orbit in his upper high-school years that foreshadowed the barrier he had yet to cope with in his upward march to world renown. Because he enjoyed singing and others appeared to enjoy listening to him, Paul went innocently to the high-school Glee Club and told the fellows he wanted to join. The others said softly that he had better not. Paul took the rebuff quietly. But who knows what roots of ambition became thus subconsciously imbedded in his soul, to nourish themselves in secret, biding their time?

Paul kept busy studying, playing ball in his free time, and working during vacations. He was bright at school, and seemed to get high grades without sacrificing other activities. His teachers encouraged him to take the com-

petitive examinations for a college scholarship. He won a
scholarship and entered Rutgers University.

When Paul entered college, he had no idea what his
vocation might be. Nobody bothered to help him make
up his mind, either. His father, although he prayed that
his sons might choose the ministry, refrained from ex-
pressing this wish. And since he had never insisted that
the boy must make a decision, Paul gave no thought to
his future. He gave himself up to the present, and had a
perfectly jolly time of it in college. One day, in his
Sophomore year, however, Paul wrote to his brother Ben,
a minister in Los Angeles, that he too had decided to study
for the ministry. By the family it was regarded as a logical
decision, especially since Paul had shown no other inclinations up to that time. Singing didn't count; that was
just fun.

Although serious about his studies, Paul was devoted to
athletics. He had a beautiful physique. The dinners of
assorted fresh garden vegetables that his father had fed
him in his childhood added up to millions of vitamins
and a strong constitution for life. Paul was sure his offer
to assist the college football team to national acclaim would
be accepted with enthusiasm. But alas, memories of the
high-school Glee Club experience rose up to haunt him.
The first week that he joined the team, the boys jumped
on him and gave him the worst thrashing of his life. He
went home beaten to the depths of his soul. He sensed
in their attack greater venom than the conventions of the
game demanded. Race, again. He told his brothers he
would resign from the team. Had not the fellows informed
him eloquently that he was superfluous? But his brothers
stood over him as he nursed his bruises and adjured, "Boy,

as soon as you're mended, you're going right back on that team and you're going to lick the stuffings out of those fellows." To make him good and mad, they accused him of being "yellow."

That was just what Paul needed. As soon as he was recovered, he went for the group that had beaten him once, and pummeled them wildly. By the time his football coach put an end to the foobtall massacre, Paul had "mended" both in body and in spirit. Coach Foster Sanford, noting his fighting spirit, determined to give him a real chance. He yanked Paul out of the scrub team and put him on the Varsity. That same year Walter Camp, national college football authority of the day, selected him for his all-American team.

Paul Robeson was nineteen and famous—as a football player. But what about his singing? He tried to join the Glee Club, but was not admitted. Because he was good at so many other things, his remarkable voice did not attract sufficient attention to overcome racial prejudice. He was collecting letters—twelve in all—in the four sports of football, baseball, basketball, and track. He was on the debating team. After winning the Freshman prize for oratory, he won the Sophomore and Junior prizes for extemporaneous speaking. To top it all, he made Phi Beta Kappa.

"Your father must have been awfully proud of Paul, to see him blazing such trails," I interjected.

"Well no," he said. "He knew what Paul could do, and he expected these honors. I remember Paul's coming home one day with a report card with seven A's and one B, and father said, 'Son, anyone who can get seven A's has no right getting a B. I expect you to erase that B.' And

Paul erased it before the next reports were issued. No matter how much other people praised Paul, father watched and criticized him if his performance dropped below his real capacity."

Paul's father died while he was in his Junior year. The boys had by this time acquired all of his best characteristics—his self-discipline, his abiding faith, his respect for individual personality and freedom, his forgiving kindness.

Toward the end of his college course, Paul confessed to his brother—the same one who gave me this story in New York—that he had lost his desire to become a minister. He wanted to try law. His brother considered how their patient father would have greeted this seeming fickleness, and patterned his reply accordingly. He merely said, "All right, boy."

"What made Paul change his mind like that?"

"I don't know for sure. For one thing, he didn't think he was good enough to preach the word of God. He told Foster Sanford, in whom he used to confide, that he often felt he lacked the necessary zeal to join the ministry. Those two went over the question of Paul's future many times before he came to me and told me he had chosen to study law."

Paul enrolled at Columbia Law School. In the summers, as usual, he worked hard and earned his tuition. When Paul finished at law school and was trying to find a clerkship, he and a musical friend, who accompanied Paul on the piano as he sang, got together and gave two or three church concerts. It was fun to sing; besides, it was a means of compensating for the non-existent income of a law-school graduate without a clerkship.

One day a friend induced Paul to go down to the local branch of the Y.M.C.A. with him, where a dramatic group

held forth regularly, with the result that Paul joined up
and took part in the presentations. At the time, this group
was interested in a manuscript by a young struggling play-
wright by the name of Eugene O'Neill. O'Neill himself
used to visit the group to watch them act. He was struck
by Paul's performance and appearance, and asked him if
he would be willing to play the role of Emperor Jones
in his new play, which was to be presented at the Provincetown Theatre, in Greenwich Village. Paul refused. Having
aspirations as a lawyer, he did not consider acting a serious
business for himself. So Eugene O'Neill offered the role
to Charles Gilpin instead. But Paul continued to interest
the Provincetown Players, who used to travel up from
Greenwich Village to the Y.M.C.A. to watch the dramatic
group in Harlem.

Perhaps the only real frustration that this brilliant and
gifted Negro ever suffered was during these years in his
early twenties when he hoped to practice law. This time his
racial origin defeated him irrevocably. Dramatics gave
him a needed outlet. At twenty-four, Paul finally consented to accept a part in *Taboo* with the Provincetown
Players. The play was a success, and the group went to
London. It was then decided to give *Emperor Jones* a
second time, and again O'Neill offered the part to Robeson. The Negro, smarting under his failure to establish a
law practice, which he still had hopes of promoting some
day, consented to fill in his spare time by taking on the
role. But there was a place in the play where he was sup-
posed to whistle, and Paul could not whistle! He tried
singing. They decided he would have to sing instead. That
is how Robeson's singing voice began to attract public
attention.

In 1925, **Paul Robeson** and **Lawrence Brown** decided to

give a concert on Sunday at the Village Theatre. They invited Heywood Broun to an advance performance. Broun was then one of the most widely read columnists in the country. He wrote enthusiastically about the coming concert in his newspaper column the next day. Much to the surprise of the two boys, when the day of the performance arrived, the regular Broadway theatergoers had come down to their tiny theater in droves and were packing the aisles. Critics opened their eyes and rubbed their ears. The next morning's newspapers hailed Broun's find as a genius. Offers came pouring in. Robeson was forced, at last, to abandon all hopes of a career as an attorney.

At twenty-two, Paul had married Eslanda Goode, a Spanish colored girl. She was a graduate of Columbia University, working as a pathological chemist at the Presbyterian Hospital. When suddenly Paul became famous as an actor and a singer, he leaned heavily upon his wife for her intelligent understanding and efficient management. In a way, she treats Paul's success much as his father did, regarding it as a natural outcome of his unusual capacity. She eggs him on to accept the full responsibility of his genius, never permitting him to rest upon past laurels.

Paul Robeson has used his gifts well. When the Fascists under Franco were making their early inroads upon the hard-won freedom of the average working man, he went to Spain and sang for the Spanish Loyalists. He sings for all oppressed people throughout the world. "I've learned," he explains, "that my people are not the only ones to be oppressed. The Jews and the Chinese receive the same treatment. Such prejudice has no place in a democracy."

Paul likes to sing the folksongs of any country, and has

studied in order to be able to sing them in their original languages. He knows Russian, Chinese, Spanish, Gaelic. "Working people sing these songs to make work easier, trying to find a way out," he says, remarkably free from race sensitiveness. Paul sent his only son to school in Russia, hoping that there he would be completely unaware of racial prejudice, at least during his childhood.

In spite of his success, and in spite of his unusual knowledge, Paul Robeson remains humble in his faith. Fame has not made him vain, but has given him a great sense of obligation, which he has accepted earnestly. "The further I go," he says, "the better it will be for my race."

That is Paul's mission.

Lenses on the World

MARGARET BOURKE-WHITE

WHEN SHE TALKS, she races. Either you gear yourself to listen at her speed, or you stay behind. Bourke-White won't wait for any man. She thrives on speed and danger. One day as she stood all alone on the roof of the United States Embassy in Russia, taking pictures of Moscow's devastations after the German attacks, a bomb exploded close by. She ducked through a window into Lawrence Steinhardt's study. The flying glass from the shattered window cut her fingers, but left her otherwise intact and free to pursue her charmed life in a violent world.

At twenty-six, Margaret Bourke-White was already considered a leading industrial photographer. Her type of work requires scientific understanding of air conditions, weather conditions, the behavior of planes in different atmospheres, the sway of steel girders on skyscrapers, and the density of the air in coal mines a thousand feet underground. Strength and endurance are the tools of her craft. While at work, she can spend sleepless nights traveling and preparing her materials. She can half freeze in sub-Arctic blizzards in Bessarabia or stew in tropical heat at the foot of the pyramids by the Nile, snatching a bite when the light is all wrong for a picture or going hungry while waiting for clouds to disappear over a choice spot of landscape. All these experiences have produced in Margaret Bourke-White, ace photographer, an air of complete co-ordination and self-assurance. Slim, straight, and lithe, she seems as intense and unmitigated as the steel and concrete she so loves to photograph. The day I met her, she was wearing something crimson, but I can't recall a line or a button of that vivid outfit. It was just part and parcel of her own striking personality.

A few odd circumstances, starting with her great-uncle's career and running through her own childhood and youth, are responsible for her lifework. As I interviewed Miss Bourke-White, I noted many of her statements and then reassembled them so that you could trace the development of a career in industrial photography.

"My great-uncle," she recalls, "was the architect who designed most of the public buildings in Dublin, of which many are still standing, so an interest in architecture runs in the family.

"My father was an inventor and worked on the designing of printing presses. But photography was a hobby of his, and often he would design something for a camera, just for the fun of it.

"As a child, I was interested in biology. I always had odd pets. One summer, I raised two hundred caterpillars. My father and I went for long walks, and he taught me a great deal about nature. He could imitate a bird so that it would come to him. I was a nature counselor at camp as a girl. In those days, I thought I would make biology my lifework. One important reason was that I wanted to travel and see the world, and I thought I could do that by going on expeditions. Well, I did get in the traveling part.

"When I went to Columbia University during my first year at college, I enrolled in an art course. As part of the course, they gave us a few hours of photography.

Clarence H. White, Senior, was the instructor, and he got me interested in the camera."

Margaret Bourke-White spent a rich childhood, but by no means an easy one. Her mother and father took their parental responsibilities very much more seriously than average parents in the neighborhood. The children were trained to make the wisest use of their time. "Mother never permitted us to play cards. She considered it a waste of time. I still don't play cards, not from any ethical reasons, but—to tell the truth—I really do find it a waste of time. I'm so glad I don't have to go in for bridge games and things like that."

Another forbidden thing in that household was the funny papers. "If I had a child," she assured me, "I would of course permit funny papers. But my mother didn't want anything to corrupt our artistic taste. She was so strict about it that she would not even permit us to visit in homes where there were funny papers."

Her father, of a scientific turn of mind, filled the house with books on science. His daughter spent many hours with him, and wanted to please him by the wise use of her leisure. "So I read his books, even though sometimes I really didn't know exactly what I was reading," she admitted. "When I read Darwin through for the first time, I'm sure I was too young to comprehend it."

But she also read the exciting, adventurous children's books. "I just adored fairy tales, especially *The Wizard of Oz*. In fact, I wrote a fan letter to the author, J. Frank Baum, when I was eight years old." (Already the aggressive energy was making itself felt.) She also read and knew the Bible, for her mother considered the Bible a great piece of classic literature. The main tenet of religious training in their home was truth. "My parents were very ethical. They brought us up to be absolutely truthful at all times."

To this day, Margaret Bourke-White insists that photography must be truthful in its depiction of life and the machine, or it is nothing. "I have no patience with the kind of camera study that will erase human lines to glamorize a face." The truth blazes forth in her pictures of people of the drought-ridden areas in the book, *You Have Seen Their Faces*. It gleams in the triumphant expressions of denial on the lined faces of Russian peasants whom she photographed during the first Five-year Plan for the book, *Eyes on Russia*, when she was but twenty-four years old. The public has come to recognize her honesty in all the camera studies she sends back to this country, snapped on the scenes of battle and turmoil the world over.

Snakes, not cameras, absorbed Margaret's interest at sixteen. During her Freshman year at college, she used to come to the art class carrying pet snakes and telling about her pet boa constrictor. After her first year at Columbia, she transferred to the University of Michigan, where she studied herpetology for two years. Then, needing money, she went to the Cleveland Museum of Natural History and asked for advice about how to proceed with her career as a biologist. The museum maintained classes for public-school children. One of the two teachers happened to be ill, and the official who interviewed Margaret Bourke-White asked whether she would be willing to substitute temporarily. Although she had no teaching certificate, she was out for work, and this seemed a good opportunity. Since the teacher in charge was ill for some time, Margaret's experience was longer than her employer had originally intended. "That was a fascinating job. I loved working with the children, the stupid ones even more than the bright ones. There was more satisfaction when you had to work harder with those who couldn't get it the first time."

Then followed two years at Cornell University, to finish and get her degree. It was during her Junior year that Margaret's father died. She was out of funds, and began to sell the pictures she had been snapping on the campus just for the fun of it. "I tried to get a job as waitress," she explained, "but there was no opening. I tried to get into the library, but they had no work for me there either. So I started to look for interesting shots around the college that I might sell." Her method was to take pictures of the common scenes in new, uncommon angles. Then came one of the biggest "breaks" in her life, to use her own words. "The pictures I took of the campus went into the Cornell alumni magazine. Some of the alumni who saw them were architects; they told me I had something unusual, and suggested that I try to sell my pictures to architects."

Despite the fact that she went to three different universities, changed her course of study, and took time out to work for a living, Margaret Bourke-White received her B.A. from Cornell at twenty, in 1927. She went straight to New York, to the office of the architectural firm of York and Sawyer, and asked to see Benjamin Moscowitz. "I went in cold, as I have usually done when applying for work of any kind."

The architect was rushing out to catch a train for Boston. With her photographs under her arm, she intercepted him at the elevator. He took one quick look, signaled to the elevator operator to go on, and went back to his office, the ingenuous college graduate running after him. Not only did he buy her pictures, but he asked for more. By this time, Margaret knew that she had something marketable to offer. "The interesting thing about that experience is that recently, after an absence of about fifteen years, the same man got in touch with me. He had been commissioned to design a building for the Lehigh Portland Cement Company in Pennsylvania, and he said, "I have saved space on the walls in the lobby for photo murals to be done by you.' I was delighted to be called on for that assignment."

Miss Bourke-White's ability attracted immediate attention. Once, when she was photographing estates in Chicago, she met the owner of one of them, the President of the Otis Steel Mill, and asked permission to go through his plant and take pictures. He gave his consent without much interest, and left for Europe. Five months later when he returned, she showed him twelve perfect shots—twelve out of a thousand that she had taken, prowling about the plant by day and night in order to find the right combination of line, mass, texture, design, and color for the most flawless camera studies. That performance meant invitations from all over the United States, Canada, Germany and Russia to photograph all the great industries of our time.

Not only does Miss Bourke-White possess amazing originality in her field, but she also uses initiative in getting her ideas launched and perseverance in carrying them out. The big industrial firms began to demand her. She became the spokesman for the machine age, one of the first to recognize its beauty. Turning her back on the objects of dead eras that other photographers were still assembling artificially before their lenses, she forced the public eye to focus on the beauty of our own dynamic times. The camera is a machine, she explains, and is thus the harmonious medium for depicting the beauty of other new machines.

To Miss Bourke-White, wheels are among the most beautiful things in the world. She once spent four days photographing a paper clip for the *American Magazine*. The paper clip, it is interesting to note, was also singled out by the industrial designer, Russel Wright, as a thing of beauty whose design is strangely analogous to the design of the modern metal-legged chair. Her type of photography is as modern a field as that of industrial design. Her work describes the structural triumphs of modern industry. The public has been laggard in understanding the creations of industrial designers. Just as an artist with his paint pots has enabled people to see and enjoy the natural loveliness of a sunset or a running brook, so Margaret Bourke-White with her eloquent photographs has opened people's eyes to mechanical beauty. Advertisements and news articles are enhanced by her pictures of functional objects.

To go back to those first years of her career: Two years after graduation, Miss Bourke-White was taken on by *Fortune* as an associate editor and sent on an assignment to Germany. But she had heard about the Five-year Plan in Russia and, being interested in factories and machinery, wanted the chance to visit a country where she could witness the beginning of an industrial movement. *Fortune* didn't want to send her there; they doubted that she would get anything worth while. So she went on her own.

"How did you hypnotize the Russian authorities into letting you, a young girl, roam through their cities at will, taking pictures?" I asked.

"I got through on the merits of some photographs I showed them. They were eager to have me take the same kind of pictures of their own industries, of which they were very proud. I got my own interpreter. She was a very capable person, who procured marvelous official papers for me. A lot depended on the kind of papers you could get. This girl was wonderful. In those early days, they didn't pay much attention to criticism from the outside. I was free to go anywhere."

That experience she put into book form in 1931. *Eyes on Russia* so pleased the Russian Government that they permitted her to come back three years later to do a second book. She is extremely fond of the Russian people, their enthusiasm, sincerity, and fine emotional power. Those qualities, she states, enabled them to wage victorious warfare on the Germans during the Second World War, for the Russian loves his country, and will gladly sacrifice his life for it. She was there at the first clash between Russia and Germany, and she says, "The women just clamored to go into the war themselves. They hate fascism and all it represents. They are idealists; they believe in their country. Everybody began volunteering to go to the front immediately, for the people are very clear on the meaning of this war. Their courage is magnificent, and they are a very sympathetic people."

Small wonder, indeed, that the Russian Government has shown Margaret Bourke-White such extraordinary hospitality. She was admitted to the Kremlin in 1940, when Harry Hopkins was sent over by President Roosevelt to talk with Stalin. The authorities, to show their trust and respect for her, ushered her through the corridors with bells ringing, and she spent an exciting time taking snapshots of Stalin standing beside Hopkins. Her comments on the experience are amusingly girlish: "Stalin stood stiffly. I wanted badly to get him sitting down, but I don't know what you can do with a dictator when he thinks he wants to stand in the middle of the room. . . ."

Miss Bourke-White listened to the Russian soldiers' comments on the shoddy apparel of their German captives —their thin helmets, poor-quality uniforms, and lack of underwear. On one of these recent treks along the Russo-German battlefront, she says that in six days she saw sixteen minutes of sunlight; for the rest there was only mud and rain.

As associate editor for *Life* these past years, Miss Bourke-White has traveled all over the world. She was in London during the blackouts and first bomb-blasting days. She went to Rumania to photograph the oil fields. In Bessarabia she worked in a blizzard. In Istanbul, Turkey, she took pictures of the President of Turkey and got herself arrested for innocently taking pictures in a Moslem temple during a prayer meeting. In Beirut, Syria, where she filmed General Weygand and the Allied forces in the Near East, she learned to ride a military camel. Thence to Egypt, to photograph the King of Egypt and the British colonial troops.

On this last-mentioned trip, Margaret Bourke-White was with Erskine Caldwell, the writer, whom she married in 1939. Together, they produced the book, *North of the Danube.* They make a good team, both in their working careers and as co-managers of their Connecticut home,

"Horseplay Hill." There Margaret shows herself to be a capable housekeeper and gardener, and a devoted wife. At the time of our interview, she was spending a good deal of her time in Darien, Connecticut, writing her new book, *Shooting the Russian War.*

Asked what it takes to be a successful photographer, she outlines these characteristics: "A sense of what is news, extreme patience, the power of observation (watch the little things) , and, above all, health and energy and light-heartedness. Even while you are in dead earnest about your work, you must approach it with a sense of freedom and joy; you must be loose-jointed, like a relaxed athlete. You must be willing to accept the most unnatural working conditions, the crazy hours, the often difficult climate, the strange, even unfriendly, environment. If you're a wo-man, getting started is hard; but once you're started, it's easier going because the fact that you're a woman attracts more attention."

"You have so often stressed good health as a prime req-uisite," I said, "What do you yourself do to maintain this?"

"Plenty of sleep. I need an awful lot of sleep, especially when I'm not working. I seem to be storing up energy. Of course once I'm on a job I can keep going on nervous energy with as little sleep as the assignment allows, and never feel tired. Aside from lots of rest, I do manage to eat well. I don't pay any attention to my figure [nor does she have to], for when I'm working hard I find that I seem to require quantities of good, nourishing food."

Margaret Bourke-White is one of the hardest working women in all the world. In her middle thirties, she con-templates a long career of gruelling activity ahead. She is engaged to give lectures, has assignments from publishers to write books, is called upon to make industrial photographs for large mechanical plants, goes off on world-wide jaunts with magazine and newspaper correspondents. Her hobby is horseback riding, a comparatively restful avocation. She also loves dancing and swimming, in fact anything that will keep her generally active. An hour spent in her society is as refreshing and invigorating as a race in a speedboat. She makes you realize the importance of an engrossing job. She is so vital and aggressive that any girl or woman would feel guilty in her presence if she too were not engaged in some serious activity as her share in the world's work.

"The Public Likes His Informality"

THE REVEREND DANIEL A. POLING

"LET'S SEE, NOW, this is 1941 and I was born about 1884, so I guess that makes me—" Dan Poling closed his eyes as he tried to master this problem in arithmetic (he said he had always hated arithmetic in school)—"about fifty-seven years old. Is that right?" He opened his eyes and thrust his massive head forward, giving me an innocent look. Bounded by wide black shadows, those eyes have an odd prophetic quality in an otherwise youthful face.

"Don't you know?" I laughed. Was this mere showmanship? I had little time to wonder, for we had barely gotten over the first friendly formalities of our meeting when the Reverend Dr. Poling was off on a formidable tirade about the long, hard fight that is still to be won against drinking. He was attempting to remain seated in the upholstered chair in a hotel room in New York, but his large frame rejected its confinement, and one leg kept sliding over one of the overstuffed arms of the chair. I noted the shock of black hair, the surcharged physique, somewhat at odds with the neat, formal dark suit.

It had been my intention to ask Dr. Poling about his early crusade for the establishment of the Eighteenth Amendment against drinking. In the course of our conversation, I had meant to say to him: "How could you, who have dedicated your life to freedom and indepen-

113

dence as the human heritage of youth, have sanctioned the passage of a law to tell a man what he may or may not personally choose to drink when, in your other activities, you have shown that you do not believe in the method of coercion to develop character?" But long before I was ready to consider the subject of prohibition, he had already described the long campaign, explaining his new approach to the problem.

"The Eighteenth Amendment failed because the law had not been preceded by a thorough educational campaign. The public won't obey a law unless they can understand the reason for it. You have to teach them the reasons for not drinking, so that they will be willing individually to make their own decisions against it. Only then will a law succeed—that is, if you still feel you want the law at all. That's the way we are working on the problem today, through the Allied Youth Organization as well as other channels."

Impelled by Dr. Poling's enthusiasm, I abandoned my outline of questions and listened as he discussed his new plans. With poise, he admitted that he had changed his own point of view. He no longer advocates the enforcement of a prohibition law as a basic step in the elimination of drinking. Undaunted by the failure of the Eighteenth Amendment, he now acknowledges the value of a better psychological approach.

Dr. Poling explained his teen-age ardor in the campaign against liquor: "You see, where I came from, out in Oregon, the liquor issue was comparable to the slave issue in the South. Drinking was associated with brawls, robbery, murder, illicit affairs. For families it meant poverty, sickness, and all kinds of physical distress. The men who had been pushing our frontier further and further toward the Western border were a wild, hard lot. They did everything more extravagantly in that part of the world. They took big chances, lived high when they had the money, behaved impulsively, and never considered the consequences. Those of us who were brought up in respectable families observed that these men were destroying every chance of happiness in their own families. Naturally, we laid much of the blame on the liquor habit and sought to clean up the West by eliminating drink."

"How old were you when you started your fight against intemperance?" I asked.

"Eighteen. While preaching in two towns in Oregon, I always brought up the subject. At twenty, I was a delegate to the National Prohibition Conference."

"Did the boys in school 'take it' from you without calling you a prig or a moralizer?"

"I suppose being popular in the athletic field helped a lot there." He did not go on to explain, but I had read that Dan Poling had collected records in Dallas College in Oregon for football, boxing, indoor diving, and track; that he was president of his class, and famous as a 'spellbinding' preacher on Sundays. As captain of the football team, he was known as "the fullback preacher" in that part of the country. He was also a newspaper reporter for the Portland *Oregonian*, a job he had held since he was sixteen. While others drew ridicule upon themselves for their temperance work, young Poling built up a following by it.

At twenty-seven, Dr. Poling—"Call me Dan"—was a candidate for Governor of Ohio, although he was too young to have held office if he had been elected. He was running on a prohibition ticket. "It was a campaign purely to elect the issue," he explained. "I spoke seven times a day for fifty-nine consecutive days in every county in Ohio, and got 47,000 votes for prohibition. The Republican candidate lost by 16,000 votes. The Republicans had refused to take on the issue of prohibition in their program. That's why I ran for Governor on the prohibition ticket. They might have had enough of those 47,000 votes to have won the election. I had shown that we had an important following. That's all I wanted."

Newspapers of the day told how young Poling had raised the prohibition vote a hundred and fifty per cent in Ohio. His was the first automobile campaign tour in the country. He carried, on this mission, an arsenal of words and a cornet player. Showmanship? Of course. But it was the only way to get a hearing for that early formulation of the temperance issue; it took into account "the personal equation." Poling has since proved that all the showmanship he employs is conceived purely for the purpose of furthering the humane causes that mean more to him than life. So utterly has he dedicated himself to a succession of fighting crusades that he appears to have lost track of the years during which he personally has grown older. That explains the mental arithmetic he had to do when I asked him his age. It was just that he hadn't thought about it for so long.

When he preached his first Thanksgiving sermon at the age of eighteen, young Poling must have been just as indifferent about his age. How else could the youth have faced undaunted a total congregation of three—a woman, her daughter, and her grandchild—who huddled together in a small, cold Evangelical church building in

Oregon? Abandoning formality, he stepped down from the pulpit and gathered his congregation to him around the old iron stove. The janitor came and gave the feeble fire a poke, but failed to add his exasperated bulk to the audience. Poling proceeded to conduct a service for the three faithfuls, displaying, in the face of odds, an informality and earnestness of purpose for which he has been distinguished throughout his career.

Poling was one of a family of nine children living on an income of four hundred dollars that his father received as a minister in Oregon. He speaks of his father as a vital personality and a remarkable man, who founded three churches and a college in Oregon. "I remember as a boy, when Father's salary was raised to six hundred dollars, that I wondered what he was going to do with all that extra money." Dan worked at ten, selling papers. The story is still told in Oregon of the time the little boy, with his newspapers under one arm, shook the hand of the immortal orator, William Jennings Bryan.

Dan had been following the crowds down the street of his town. A holiday had been declared in order that everyone might go to hear Bryan. The speaker's carriage was roped off, but the little boy ducked under the ropes and climbed up on the rear axle just as Bryan started to speak. There he perched precariously throughout the thrilling address, his mouth open in admiration. Bryan was a Democrat; Dan, the son of a Republican. Even at his age, the boy could see how Bryan's matchless oratory was breaking through the political prejudices of that audience. "I could feel his power. He spoke so that even a boy like myself could understand and be moved. He had just finished a campaign against McKinley, the Republican

candidate who had won the Presidency. He was telling
us all that, now that the election had put a Republican
in the White House, it was up to us to back that man, no
matter to what party we belonged. I admired him for
that as much as for his oratory. Then, as he finished his
speech, he naturally turned around to shake hands with
the men who had been standing beside him. I stuck out
my hand. It so happened that when his hand went out,
mine was the first he grasped, and he shook it warmly. We
were equals, we two men! I never forgot that moment.
And the whole town talked about it." Bryan and Poling
were to become great friends in later years, although
politically they remained worlds apart.

That incident may have had something to do with Dan's
interest in oratory. In any event, he practiced seriously in
his early adolescence, winning a speaking contest in the
State of Oregon. Born of seven generations of clergymen,
preaching seemed a natural step. Dan was also well known
in his state as an athlete. When he started to preach at
eighteen, he became famous locally for his "muscular
Christianity." Another of Poling's ambitions was to be a
writer. "You know," he deprecated, "everybody wants to
write the great American novel some day. Well, so did
I." Among other things, he wrote four novels. One of
these, *The Furnace,* tells of the famous United States Steel
strike of 1910.

Poling, through his associate directorship in the World
Interchurch Movement, had served with a group who investigated the labor conditions that caused the men to
strike. The facts they secured were gathered into a report.
Poling explained his share in the work: "As a member of
the Committee of three entrusted with the task of liquidat-

ing the activities and materials of the Interchurch World Movement at the close of the program of that organization, I had special responsibilities in bringing out this report." It covered two printed volumes and had a wide circulation. The Interchurch group became interested originally in alleviating the problem of the twelve-hour day, but the final report went much further than that. It developed into a critique of the American social-industrial system. It covered the seven-day week, the spy systems of great corporations, the selfish irresponsibility of some of labor leadership, the biased press, the inert pulpit, the hegemony of the United States Steel Corporation over the anti-union forces of the nation, and the partisan anti-democratic acts of some government officers in denying civil rights. The two books containing the whole grim story were circulated widely among colleges, churches, forums, and the press.

Only a man with unusual audacity and indifference to his own personal popularity dared to champion the cause of labor in those days. Compared to England, America was a backward country as regards the rights of labor. Men like Poling were fighting an unpopular cause; their position on the labor issue threatened their careers. It took great faith and courage on the part of these Interchurch leaders to conduct that investigation and follow it with a wide distribution of the facts. But Poling went even further in this crusade, writing a long denunciation of the United States Steel Corporation shortly thereafter because of their failure to take up the challenge to improve labor conditions. In 1920, he published an article on the subject entitled, "Still Silent on the Twelve-hour Day," from which I quote: "Far over 100,000 workers still rise in the dark, work twelve hours, go home in the dark, isolated in steel plants from family and nation. What may we expect the attitude of these to be toward the Church, the press, the government and all else that constitutes 'public opinion'—if only a great silence meets the cry of their bondage?"

These words explain why Poling has been active on behalf of so many social causes. He believes that the Church has a responsibility toward our social order. His is no mere Bible-quoting religious leadership. Poling has had the real satisfaction in ensuing years of seeing the changes take place, one by one, for which he fought in his youth. His face lit up happily as he gave me the final sequel to this episode in his career: "And do you know, by 1935 we had the gratification of seeing the last of all the recommendations of that Interchurch report put into effect by Myron Taylor. It was the acceptance of the principle of collective bargaining." Poling, who had worked in a steel mill in his teens, lifted his shoulders expressively as he told of the lightening of the steelworkers' burdens. He searches out the hornets' nests of social ills, but even as he uncovers them, his faith in man keeps growing, for he takes deep delight in each separate triumph of good over evil.

Dr. Poling told me an interesting story about John D. Rockefeller, Junior, that illustrates his eagerness to seek and give credit to a man's best impulses. As Rockefeller was a major owner in the United States Steel Corporation, Poling naturally expected to face obstruction and antagonism from that quarter. This is what he actually encountered: "Originally, Rockefeller did not favor the investigation. He felt that it was outside the field of the Interchurch World Movement, which was not organized or equipped to specialize in such matters. However, when the investigation was authorized, and after the report had been completed, he *insisted* that the report be printed and released to the public. There was strong opposition within the Executive Committee of the Interchurch World Movement. I do not believe the Executive Committee would have authorized the release of the report had Mr. Rockefeller not insisted as he did. It was a demonstration of the free and fair-mindedness of this remarkable Christian man."

Once, in an earlier investigation, Dan Poling had directed his faith in human beings toward an injustice against a great mass of people. During the First World War, rumors began to spread in this country to the effect that the American soldiers were behaving disgracefully abroad. Poling, who went to France with the American Young Men's Christian Association as an active pacifist, questioned these rumors. He resented their effect on the people back home; but more than that, he was angered because of the reverberations over in the trenches and in the hospitals, where he had opportunity to observe the boys at first hand. He worked tirelessly in the front lines on his regular assignment with the Young Men's Christian Association contingent. But in the midst of his labors, touched by the high morale of the United States Army, he found time to make a study and submit a comprehensive report on the behavior of the American soldiers on foreign soil that effectively repudiated the evil rumors and was gratefully accepted by Secretary of War Newton D. Baker. In this report, published in 1918 under the title, *Physically Competent and Morally Fit*, Poling said: "The psychology of such charges is demoralizing. Confidence begets confidence. Men are made strong by the knowledge that other men believe in them. . . . I found the American in uniform . . . resenting indulgence that causes his country's civilization to be misjudged; he is disciplining his comrade; . . . he shows a distinct pride in the fact that American physical and moral standards are high. . . . He is a representative American and he is living on a moral plane which is above the moral plane of civilian life at home." Poling was still a youth when he wrote those words, but his humane, Christian outlook appears strongly developed, and the style of his writing is mature. The report became the basis for his book, *Huts in Hell*.

In 1923, Poling was asked to become pastor of the Marble Collegiate Church in New York. It was the first and only time in its history of three hundred years that the church had offered the pastorship to a man who had not attended a theological seminary. Poling had an M.A. from Dallas College; it was only after this appointment that he received his D.D. Since then he has piled up enough degrees to satisfy the most orthodox respecter of academic letters. But he is still "Dan Poling," informal, friendly, bursting with energy, and the friend of young people. Thousands came to hear his short, earnest sermons, made without notes, before he resigned from the Marble Collegiate Church in 1929. His work as president of Christian Endeavor had grown to such proportions that he needed to clear the decks for this leadership on behalf of the world's youth.

Dr. Poling still held on to his job as editor in chief of the *Christian Herald,* however, which he had acquired in 1927. At that time, he gathered about him a staff of young writers and proceeded to boost the circulation of the paper

by almost one hundred per cent. Since then, the paper
has added to its responsibilities the execution of four welfare projects, which it finances with the help of its sub-
scribers. It supports a children's home, the Bowery Mission in New York, a memorial home for aged religious
workers and their wives in Florida, and a charitable project in China. More than a newspaper, the *Christian
Herald* is a medium through which Dr. Poling promotes
his many worthy causes. It co-ordinates his own program
and that of his vast following. At the present writing, the
paper is concerned with organizing for peace when this
war is over. No other religious publication enjoys so
wide a circulation.

In his service to youth, Poling has often used the question-and-answer technique. As early as 1926, he ran a
radio program that included a youth conference service.
He answered questions on religion, morals, philosophy,
and health. Some of those questions were humdingers,
but with patience and good humor he took on all comers.
He had had a long apprenticeship in this technique during
the years when he edited a question-and-answer column
of the Portland *Oregonian,* in his early twenties. Later,
when he conducted a weekly vocational-guidance service
on the air, he amassed a whole new following. Poling
does not hedge when confronted with a difficult problem
but says what he thinks, and, because he is honest, wise,
and never belligerent, one is impressed by his opinions.
He knows about youth in the family as well as through
his leadership of the world organization, for he is the father
of eight children. The last one he adopted; she is an English girl, orphaned by the First World War.

As international president of the largest youth organi-

zation in the world, Christian Endeavor, Dr. Poling makes
his strongest appeal to youth. Young people like him
because he has faith in them and asserts this faith at all
times. On a weekly radio program, he carries forward
his championship of youth through the network. He believes young people are "as intrinsically fine today as they
have ever been, that we are getting out of our investment
in them vastly more than we deserve. . . . Youth today is
essentially sound." He believes that youth is now having
a greater struggle than in previous decades and is making
a better showing for itself. As a professional observer of
youth, he ought to know. Christian Endeavor has an all-
inclusive program. It stands for world peace, religious
Christian education and adherence, unity of the churches,
and good citizenship. It has co-ordinated the eighty Protestant faiths and seeks to promote a co-operative Christian
service. This aim Dr. Poling pursued for many years
through his former position as director of laymen's activities in the Interchurch World Movement. There he fought
for more than mere denominational consolidation. He
used to say that, in his boyhood, he had learned that there
was no use trying to tie a shock of corn together at the
bottom; the first tying had to be at the top. "Whatever
the future of any faith, the future of Protestantism is either
hopelessly—or hopefully—identified with Protestant unity."
For this he had tried to enlist the interest of men and
women alike, believing that the practice of leaving the
religious direction of a family to the mothers alone is un-
fair and ineffective.

Poling's boundless energy has been drawn upon still
further in the past few years. Although a member of the
Dutch Reformed Church, he was asked to become pastor

of the Baptist Temple in Philadelphia in 1936, and accepted. As leading advocate for church co-ordination, this denominational difference troubled him not at all. In this office he succeeded the famous Russel Herman Conwell, noted for his sermon, "Acres of Diamonds," which was delivered 6,152 times. Dr. Poling was offered this appointment while he was on the last lap of a six-year world tour that he had undertaken in order to organize the various national unions of Christian Endeavor. He now travels back and forth between New York and Philadelphia each week, not to mention his major jaunts around the world by plane. He has flown over 438,000 miles and speaks with nostalgic pride of the time when, for three years, he owned his own plane.

Poling is a peace-loving man, but he takes issue with those who would impose their pacifism on younger members of our society by extracting pledges of them. He has written: "For me there is a certain immorality in pledging a specific action in advance of a particular event the details of which cannot be known. For me to so pledge shuts the door of choice in the face of conscience and destroys, or may destroy, both intellectual freedom and intellectual honesty."

When a youthful member of the Christian Endeavor Movement says, "In my whole life everywhere I will be Christian," he is motivated by the highest impulses in the face of any eventuality, but he is free to "rethink his position" instead of being strangled by earlier pronouncements made in the midst of a different set of circumstances. Many a pacifist, confused and disillusioned by what has happened to the pacifist pledgees in light of the recent world conflict, will take heart at these courageous words.

Poling seeks no issue with pacifists; he considers himself one. His issue is with those who unfairly coerce youth into making pledges that involve lifelong commitments. His own particular form of pacifism he describes adequately in the chapter of a book published in 1941, *Youth Marches,* entitled, "There Is an Answer to War." The book as a whole is beautifully written and very moving, and it reveals the philosophical development of the "fullback preacher" since he made his maiden sermon in a small town in Oregon, at the age of eighteen.

All things, great and small, seem worthy of Dr. Poling's time. His major concerns are his pastorship, a weekly radio series, the presidency of Christian Endeavor, editorship of the *Christian Herald,* and his affiliation with Allied Youth. He may also be writing a novel or poetry on the side, or painting pictures, miraculously ferreting out moments of leisure for these hobbies. What he will do next is anybody's guess.

Dr. Poling magnetizes crowds, who back his every venture in the cause of Christianity. In his faith in people lies his great strength. Few men have exerted so profound an influence on American and world youth.

"Textbook Stuff"

THE SUGGESTION WAS MADE that with this book I might submit a discussion plan to be used by leaders of young people's groups. The ten chapters might comprise a "course" in human conduct, and groups would be encouraged to analyze the biographical sketches and pick out the moral and religious impulses by which each famous youth was motivated.

The manuscript, during the entire process of preparation, was submitted to groups of young people for their criticism. I asked them how they would like a section devoted to "discussion outlines" on the chapters. "Nerts!" they hurled at me. "Poison!" And worst of all, "Textbook stuff!"

But when I promised to make this section short and snappy, they said all right provided I made sure to stow it away in an appendix, which they hardly ever bother to look at anyway.

Here in the appendix, therefore, I hide my suggestion for a discussion outline to go with the sketches. They are a few sample questions and statements that might lead off a group at a forum on such popular youth group subjects as "Choosing One's Lifework," "Religion in Today's World," "Getting Along with People," or "Using Your Talents."

1. Were the persons in these sketches seeking fame? What were they aiming for?

2. Consider the changes they made in their plans. Were they wise? What mistakes did they make? How were their careers affected by the way in which they handled mistakes?

3. Analyze the personal conduct of the characters. Are they careful about health and behavior, more than the average? Give examples.

4. Describe the place of religion in the lives of these persons. How did their actions express their religious convictions?

5. How did their achievements help their fellow men?

6. How did the following handicaps affect their careers: physical defect; illness; racial prejudice; poverty; death of a parent; environmental conditions; other handicaps?

7. What do you consider your own best talent? What do you do to develop it? How do you plan to use it for the common welfare?

8. What are your handicaps? How do you tackle each? To what extent have you lowered your standard of achievement for yourself because of them? How has a handicap made you accomplish more?